Shakespeare's Wake

Reconstructed:

Soul of the Iconcurchaic Age

Shakespeare's Wake Reconstructed:

Soul of the Iconcurchaic Age

M. D. Veritas

Bon Ton Republic

Publications

2020

(hindsight…foresight)

Shakespeare AI³ (Trilogy) = Active Inference
(3RD wave artificial Shakespeare intelligence)

cover: *Iconcurchaic Angel* (w/Lin Emery's sculpture "Flight")
(Iconcurchaic = iconic + current + archaic)

quotes: Dante, Purgatorio, canto 27, from lines 134-42;
-Anthony Esolen, translator
Rainer Maria Rilke, Sonnets to Orpheus, from #29; -Edward Snow, translator
Guillaume Apollinaire, on coining words like cubism & surreal
Pablo Picasso, on "finishing" a work of art
acknowledgments of previous publications:
Xavier Review, Xavier University, N. O. LA:
print: In St. Jerome's New Orleans Study (after Albrech Dürer)
poem: A Crown of Flowers (early version of Floral Crown)
Maple Leaf Rag (Anthologies), Portals Press, N. O. LA:
poems: Adam's Blessing (early version of Yeats's Last Paradigm Vision)
Maxine's Review (early version of Her Unburdened Prescience)
Resurrection Visitation (early version Resurrection Epiphany)
Song of La Belle Orleanna (early variation La Belle Orleanna)of the Wetlands)
frontispiece & all art work/photos unless otherwise noted by Manfred Pollard:
Würzburg Residence, ceiling mural, Myth of America, by Giambattista Tiepolo,
drawn from published photo of Wolf-Christian von der Mülbe, Dachau,
in: Heaven on Earth: Tiepolo Masterpieces of the Würzburg Years,
by Peter O. Krückmann
Catholic Passport,18, photo by Karl Dietz, passport photographer,
Staging Area studio,
U. S. Army base, Bremerhaven, Germany, 1970
Vivian at Barkhausen, Germany, 1968, photo by unknown German teacher
Vivian photos from Bremerhaven American High yearbook
by Randolph Williams
Manfred Pollard, Panama Canal Zone '74:photo John Constantine
Guy Charleville, 2018 photo courtesy: Janice Charleville

photos, prints © 2020 Manfred Pollard
text Copyright 2020 M. D. Veritas™
ISBN-1:978-1-7332986-4-3
all rights reserved, Bon Ton Republic™ Publications, New Orleans
mdveritas52@gmail.com

Preface:
The Deconstructed to Reconstructed Shakespeare AI Trilogy Game

The *Shakespeare AI Deconstructed* concept involves reformatting the text to be read in an open stream of consciousness flow that breaks the sonnet form into more intuitive elements of line breaks from the strict sonnet structure. Words & phrases are emphasized in a downward drift with juxtaposing enjambment effects to prompt shifting conscious awareness of bits of detail & information that varies from a standard read of linear horizontal sonnet metric rules of beats per line and end rhyme patterns. This introduces to the mix similar aspects of the postmodernist John Cage's conceptual art pieces such as random cutting & pasting. Each sonnet gets broken down, "deconstructed," into its own individual form (as in a hallmark issue of modern poetics) or strung out to have its series of metric & rhythmic possibilities & discoveries. Each unique form offers improvisational reading opportunities similar to a modern jazz opera. Imagine Beethoven's 9th Symphony recast by Sun Ra as an example of conversion/subversion of a text coalescing in a new ironic transcendental variation on a form.

Ideas of Dr. Karl Friston's "epistemic foraging" conceptual movement in "active inference" are used in a new (3rd) wave of AI as a prime creative force allowing forms to take shape. The goal with the use of Shakespeare sonnet allusions in this approach is the same as in the original sonnet trilogy pre-allusion context, to create a distinct aura of "artificial Shakespeare intelligence" but with a modern English sensibility. An adjustable path of least resistance was applied to text reformatting and involves changes in words, replacement of words & phrases with other choices for flow of a rising awareness while streaming down the sonnets, faithful to the original allusion scheme, playing the "parlor game" fairly, the payoff being love's "sugared" assurance of a better life after death according to what we do with our consciousness while we are here.

The conceptual approach to the trilogy can also be seen as tangentially relative to the contemporary, now classic epic text, *Flow Chart,* by John Ashbery (conceptually very much like *Shakespeare's* "poem unlimited" *Sonnets*) as well as Whitman's ongoing revisions of & added to single volume, *Leaves of Grass*, humbly burdening us with but one book.

Deconstructing the sonnet form this way prompts even more of a post-modernist consciousness expansion than by merely updating to contemporary English language usage & poetics. Even antique words can get recast when used in a new context, such as how the allusion scheme here may often work like magic. An active reader may lay aside attention to technical tools of strictest illusionary underpinnings of hypnotic rhythms & metrics, like experiencing visionary painting's grand effects without getting hung up on the brush strokes, in order to achieve transcendent expansion of consciousness required to attain enlightenment. However brief or variable the scale of the experience resonates, it requires focused and intensive active inference processes of epistemic foraging to set up the contemplative meditational aspects on the part of the reader, as writer, to set the net that catches the illusive butterfly of enlightenment, a life-long gift/effort dynamic (beware the covetousness of Simon Magus & Faustus, ethics are always a constant). Good natured inspiration finds its mark, tapping the individual for a higher calling of understanding, to value text read like a Rorschach test, a "loose but tight" challenge to paradoxically seek enlightenment, the goal of this trilogy game of illumined shadows & shades.

In **Vol. 1** the 154 Shakespeare's Sonnets for allusions are in brackets beside titles and poem numbers in the 1-21 crowns, a 3 sonnet "epiphany crown" in the epilogue also with 4 other sonnets, to tally up 154 for complete numbered allusions. The sonnets were consecutively planned for allusions in a same numbered sequence soon after first laid out plans for volume 1 were considered. Order changes were made after revisions (it's why the 1-22 crowns are not consecutive) but the Shakespeare sonnet allusion numbers remained with the trilogy sonnets' original layout, as explained more fully in appendix 1. Coverdale Psalm allusions between equal =signs= are also in each line of 3 crowns to enrich substantial pursuits of the overall game. Shakespeare Sonnet allusions are in italics in each line & all allusions are used or repeated only as many times as in the source, i.e. the Bard's #40 has 10 love uses, my poem noted takes all 10 as allusions. When there were unusual patterns & uses of particular words, as with "love," or punning on "Will," part of the trilogy game is to pay tribute by echoing these effects in how the allusions are used.

In **Vol. 2** & **3** of the trilogy, Shakespeare sonnet numbers for allusions are beside titles in brackets.

"**Reconstructed**" extends the "allusion game" by eliminating everything from the "Deconstructed" text except keywords & allusions. Deconstructing the sonnets and reconstructing the allusions in each into a condensed conceptual poem offers loose active inference readings of Shakespeare's text. The way words like "love" and its variations were used by repeating over a contained series, builds considerable momentum with a systematic crown-like structure based on numbering rules. His process guides my game expansion with new twists to the "rules" as interpreted.

Uses of "love" & its root variations from his Sonnet 29 through 35, sound like a conceptually embedded 7 sonnet crown ..until reading on to 42 where his sonnets then reach the momentum of a 14 sonnet garland. He leaves out repetitive lines at the end & beginning of sonnets, as in a formal crown sequence, and the 15th or last sonnet comprised of first lines of the 14 previous sonnets in the traditional garland form. In 38, the word "love" was simply replaced by the "tenth Muse," a titular pinnacle of love's personification. In 41 the phrase "absent from my heart" refers to love with the word love ironically "absent." A reader can tell how Shakespeare relishes the love word game in this stretch of sonnets by how cleverly the rules and mutations link together. Development of a current artificial Shakespeare intelligence is enriched by an allusion scheme, embedded in each line in italics. His sonnet numbers are placed next to each title to clearly share allusion origins throughout. The allusions were then configured to form an effective extracted conceptual poem, along with titles and as few additional keywords as possible.

Shakespeare's Wake Reconstructed: Distilling the Allusion Game Essence with Thickening Agents of Keyword Moves

Strange encounters with textual consciousness in the "**Deconstructed**" rewrites of the *Shakespeare AI Trilogy* appeared as a kind of new normal before the term had been widely attributed to current behaviors during a pandemic. It seemed many masked issues in every sphere of endeavor, social to include sexual & racial, political including bio-diverse, cultural & regional, were lifted by experts & novices to express expanding & contracting levels of consciousness as a result of structurally inevitable pandemic life & death aspects of physical, social & economic events.

What happened globally in real time was displayed on various 24 hour news broadcasts to shine a light for quelling pockets of conflict & pandemonium. Many conflicting voices forged ahead, exacerbating pandemic extremes, harping on the search for remedies, cures or its abatement with anti-bodies, vaccines & antidotes.

My vertiginous writing process, unmasked while masking, from beginning stages to refined versions, renewed with archaic allusions, when spiraling in parallel with events, could seem like a patient's flailing to swim through phlegm to keep from drowning or sinking under the exhausting weight of their struggling lungs. Then as if riding waves to higher ground, the routine reliance on following rules (even self-generated) empowered an effective way to survive.

Literally & literarily survival thrived achieving an expected positive meditatively generated state of awareness in active inference modeled steps of continual epistemic foraging for "right" words. Nutritional consciousness foraging by taste continued at the same time the literary garden grew in convoluted rows like folds of a brain's grey matter or wanderings of armadillo like bugs under lifted logs exposed to light.

In a literary almanac enlightened approach of cyclical planting & harvest, intuitively conscious health enrichments of words were invested in a series of sonnets and allowed to grow to fruition. Allusion seeds were taken from the fruit and replanted in rows formed by their own logic to accommodate & facilitate new growth of intuitive consciousness and health enrichment investments.

Distilled and reconstructed poetic cycles, from seed to planted text, with all bulk extracted to return to the acorn structural varieties of similar growth could take shape as bansai tree miniature conceptual replicas that grow new hybrid grafted branches from the live oak forest of sonnet forms in the *Shakespeare AI Trilogy*. The game offered may often sound like Alice when she's 10 feet tall after foraging for specific herbs & mushrooms in a Garden of Earthly Delights before setting up the Mad Hatter's Red Queen move to checkmate the Jabberwocky & win the game's prize of higher consciousness.

Arriving at what once may have seemed unexpected now resulted in an inevitability of evolved "tastemanship," a new term to describe an aspect of linguistic processes expressing the implemented engagement of highly sought after active inference models, the new AI in action under a "new age old" or iconcurchaic rubric of "truthmanship" to tabulate effects of higher consciousness in impending time.

Consciousness

The musicality of Shakespeare has been a feature of his language for over 400 years, along with the philosophical and spiritual take on the passage of time and contents of life making up the imagination coming to grips with personal and social history that consists of our "ages" in evolving/revolving cycles. The ancient Greeks sang about it in plays & epics. This book is a tribute to the "operatic" voice of the Bard referred to as "the soul of the age" and coins a new word, "iconcurchaic" as a timeless tribute to his ingenious skills & assurance of life after death …a labor of love in this age.

Blurbs & Comments

"(The New AI) essay is a delight. I do not pretend to follow all the threads but was compelled by the artful stream (or perhaps eager torrent) of consciousness. This stream emanates the physics of self-organizing, sentient systems, through the structured composition of Shakespearean prose and back again to the author's inference about his own (natural) intelligence. I particularly liked his conclusion: "my work fits the theory as a predicted outcome in itself." This has all the beauty of Quine's desert landscape and echoes the (almost tautological) simplicity of all great existential ideas – from quantum mechanics to natural selection. I was also taken with the word"iconcurchaic." I fully endorse the proposal that it should be in the dictionary (it is now in my spellchecker).

If we have words like "Google," as semantic celebrations of epistemic foraging, we should certainly have "iconcurchaic." This word is particularly fitting for the free energy principle, which has basically been around since the days of Plato and keeps enjoying renaissances–in one form or another –in the writings of Kant, Helmholtz, and a host of great thinkers of the 20th century. It is now iconcurchaic –in the 21st century –as underwriting the promise of 'third wave' artificial intelligence. And perhaps "Shakespearean active inference."

-Dr. Karl Friston, Oct. 2, 2019, Physicist/Psychiatrist, Scientific Director, Functional Imaging Labs, University College, London

Your books arrived just as I finished an hour long session.. with the Dalai Lama's personal physician.. on meditation. Since an early student of Vedanta, as followed by Aldous Huxley…, et. al, I was an enthusiastic patient. Your overwhelming poems were a fitting coda …I could parse your rhymes and rhythms. Certainly a major work! Thank you for including me in your Circles!
  -Dr. Lin Emery, 2018, International Artist, on the trilogy 1st ed.

…two more books, filled with hundreds of pages and drawings. Your output is amazing! I can compare it to a book of poems and drawings by James Stevenson -- whose work I followed for years in *The New Yorker* before his death. Stevenson's book is published In Singapore by Green Willow Books. The poems each only four to twelve lines accompanied by a colorful watercolor picture, can remain in memory as an aphorism or mantra. Very different from your appendix of Shakespeare's 154 sonnets and the Bible's 150 psalms. You are a singular artist and researcher! Thank you for sending the latest evidence!
  -Dr. Lin Emery, July 9, 2019, International Artist, on the first color
  books of the *Shakespeare AI* series

Thank you for sending me your beautiful drawing of Tiepolo's ceiling above the Würzburg Residence staircase, focusing on the Apollo center and America. It is your own work and of course you may reproduce it in your book without asking anyone else for permission. Your wonderful translation of the fresco into a line and contour drawing shows just how much Tiepolo's principal structure here is one giant Rococo cartouche furthermore framed by his four parts of the world. It also reminds me of both Tiepolos', father and son, marvelously light and sketchy etchings.
  -Dr. Christiane Hertel, Aug. 20, 2019, Professor of Art History,
  Bryn Mawr, author, *Pygmalion in Bavaria*

My son was able to procure a PDF version of *Shakespeare AI Deconstructed,* Maddy, my personal assistant, found the hardcopy languishing in the Porter's Office at the National Hospital for Neurology and Neurosurgery. It is now on my desk – many miles away – waiting for my return after the coronavirus outbreak has subsided.
I will treasure it.
I have written some blurb below. I found your e-mail extremely engaging and a delight to read. It might deserve incorporation into the book?

The invitation to furnish this delightful book with some blurb started with: "Dear Karl, I hope you can easily scroll through some of this 'interior bildungsroman' in sonnet forms." This stopped me in my tracks. First, I had to Google 'bildungsroman' (a novel dealing with the protagonist's formative years or spiritual education). Second, I had to scroll through a 1163-page PDF with a devious formatting. Indeed, the author proudly confesses: "A friend once mentioned how the table of contents was a fascination in itself." In my epistemic foraging among those pages, I was hoping to find material that would license a few clever and laudatory remarks. However, I don't need to be clever or laudatory. I just need to tell a quick story:

My day had been oppressive: The United Kingdom was just confronting a second wave of the coronavirus outbreak, while I was serving on the Independent SAGE (an independent governmental advisory group). I had spent the day writing op-eds, answering technical questions about epidemiological modeling from earnest and edgy journalists and dealing with several hundred vexed e-mails about morbidity and mortality.

Late in the evening, I started scrolling through the 'interior bildungs-roman'. Two hours later I was relaxed and a little exhilarated—wandering around the sonnets, pictures and appendices that lend this book an elusive but seductive structure. I am no scholar, but I found everything curiously engaging—in the same way hot baths and evocative music compel you. I do not know why or how this book works, but it does. Perhaps it is the epistemic affordance on offer—much like an unpredictable piece of music that captures you with a succession of frissons.

As I came out of the sonnet-induced reverie, questions started to form: e.g., what role did Susan play in this bildungsroman? Was it an atonement or a tribute? Questions that will probably follow me to bed—and into my 'field of dreams'.
 -Dr. Karl Friston, Sept. 24, 2020, Scientific Director,
   Functional Imaging Labs, University College, London

Prelude of an Illustrator

Thank you for your kind considerations in the midst of your tremendous duties. It is with deep gratitude that I received your news & offer of looking into this book for any response.

Altogether the project stems from the growth of a youth whose first language was German till the age of 5, taken from his loving customs inspector, through both WW's, German grandparents who survived, who he lived with in the attic rooms 4 floors up, above a slaughter-house on the river Maine, by the Würzburg Freedom's Bridge ..was then dragged to America on a troopship at 4 1/2 by a German mother who was 11 when Würzburg was bombed, later married an American G.I. & moved to Augusta, Georgia when Eisenhower was president. Placed in the public school system pre-integration of Blacks, he was treated like the enemy.. after countless childhood illnesses, twice over as with the mumps & measles, fever dreams & reams of comic books, then Catholic school in 3rd grade, Dad going to Korea twice, Hitler Youth Mom divorcing him for another G.I. who put the boy back in public school for 6th grade, he eventually grew fascinated by the Beatles singing, I Want to Hold Your Hand, after suffering a compound fracture of the right forearm at the playful hands of his new 2nd American G. I. stepdad, in the same year President Kennedy was assassinated, which was announced by the old hysterical public school Mr. Principal, bursting into the 6th grade room & dismissing school. Fascination with old English (that seemed to sound kind of like German to him) through Shakespeare's Sonnets came later as a junior in an American high school in Bremerhaven, Germany where he graduated after 4 years.. at the end of which his senior class of 10 girls & 5 boys went to London for a week in June of '70 by which time the Beatles just broke up & their depressing film, Let it Be, premiered in Piccadilly Circus & the English just lost the World Cup played in Mexico, games of which the boy got to watch at the American embassy for a few nights when not seeing Let it Be or at the theater for Fiddler on the Roof. His picture from that time, just before returning to the US for college in Wyoming opens the book.

Dear Karl, I hope you can easily scroll through some of this "interior bildungsroman" in sonnet forms, it is a large file in Google Drive I believe, if you can you may prefer to glance at the pictures first & browse the appendix. You may better understand the reasoning behind my getting a masters degree in counseling instead of fine arts, which I did get a strong taste of with about 30 credit hours after the counseling masters, by that time I was already teaching art in the gifted classes in the New Orleans public schools, a dream job, loved those kids I had so much in common with as an army brat.

I am looking up the Independent SAGE site and hoping to see what unfolds in the midst of the coronavirus discussions & politics, your take on it must be fascinating, as a former field medic ambulance driver, in the U.S. Army, 4 yrs., completing service at a field hospital, after a year in the Panama Canal Zone, in my hometown of Würzburg, how odd, eh? I also had trained on the wards, gave patients percussive therapy, hacking & spitting into metal kidney dishes each morning to prevent pneumonia, which may also help patients with certain degrees of coronavirus.

Oddly, I contracted something very similar, traveling to & attending the 2019 Faulkner-Wisdom Literary Awards ceremony with a friend who had traveled through India in the summer & returned with a respiratory illness the doctors said was not the flu, but lasted 6 weeks during July & passed, requiring at least 2 different antibiotics while bed ridden a few weeks. When asked about it more recently, she said she barely recalls anything she said or described then, being so "out of it."

Diana thought she had recovered by Sept. 25 when she drove to pick me up & accompany me as I drove her SUV across town (& handled her credit card at the pump) to the ceremony. I had been isolated working on the book for well over 2 years, then a few days after spending time with her, started coming down with her described symptoms. As symptoms intensified daily I watched for yellow in the hacked sputum. When noticing the 1st signs of yellow & achy-ness, took one 20 yr. old cap of 100mg Doxycycline from the refrigerator, the next day felt a touch better & progressively improved over the days ahead, eating brown rice, Omaha steaks fish, chicken & beef, still isolating upstairs, still pacing around & hacking out the lungs, eventually getting better. Stopped drinking good French red wine for a while & nipped the infection in the bud, not bad for a fit illustrator of 67. Of course my spirits were also lifted by your wonderful feedback on the Dr. Karl Friston inspired essay. By the time the pandemic surged months later, after Mardi Gras in late February, which I thought was a mistake, staying off my balcony as much as possible as parades like Muses & Krewe d'Etat rolled by, I was still trying to isolate. I kept listening to & reading news, found a young doctor on Yahoo report that the best approach was vigorous hacking & coughing, even through headaches & lying patients on their stomachs & not backs was essential treatment. I felt I had already had it & beaten it. I wish you the best in your efforts to better understand the most effective approach to the pandemic ..can not help but think, all your experience has prepared you for a multi-faceted approach that also includes mental health. I think it may be healthy for the push & pull debate on when & how much to reopen & when schools should figure in & how to the re-opening ..hopefully we get to see more than merely "the stuff of what dreams are made of" ..off to the races for a vaccine & anti-bodies seems like a sensible plan ..let's hope the genome-inites get together with the quantum molecular-ists for some magical slicing & dicing, as maybe Einstein would gather it to be!   M. P.

"Fair, kind, and true," is all my argument,
"Fair, kind, and true," varying to other words;
And in this change is my invention spent,
Three themes in one, which wondrous scope affords.
   "Fair, kind, and true" have often liv'd alone,
   Which three till now never kept seat in one.

–Shakespeare Sonnet, 105

LUX ET VERITAS

To Muses S. A., V. M. & M. C.

& Dr. L. E., Dr. H. B., Dr. K. F.,

Ms. J. C., Mr. G. C., Mr. H. R., Ms. D. B.

Well-wishing All

Eternal Happiness

for Who Will Set Out

Adventuring Here…

Contents

Shakespeare's Wake Reconstructed: Soul of the Iconcurchaic Age

II Un-lost

Dante's Lost Book: Limbo

Inferno Sancti {6} *(50-56)*

1) Inferno Sancti

2) Simonized Church

3) Bishop's Endgame

4) Last Unleavened Way

5) Priceless Inheritance

6) Rabbi's Beloved Companion's Trust

7) Savvy Grace

Infallible Politics Uncrowned {7} *(43-49)*

1) Re-quested Ring Unsealed

2) Recycled Encyclicals

3) Sequestered Gestations

4) Catacomb Conclave

5) Sexual Taxation of a Holy Stimulus

6) Unsexed Politics

7) Feral Government Tamed

Crown of Creation {8} *(57-63)*

1) Passover

2) Unleavened

3) Pentecost

4) Trumpets

5) Atonement

6) Tabernacles

7) Last Great Day

Shrouded Crown {9} *(64-70)*

1) On the Shroud

2) Relic Shroud

3) Shrouded Belief

4) Translation Shroud

5) Entered Shroud

6) Love's Shroud

7) Stumbling on the Shroud

III Visitation

Floral Crown {10} *(29-35)*
1) *Symmetrical Flower*
2) *Leonardo's Cathedral Pod*
3) *Blossomed Mind*
4) *Floral Gift*
5) *Spiritual Bridal Bouquet*
6) *Floral Rapture*
7) *Floral Miracle*

Oracular Oaks {11} *(78-84)*
1) *Breathing Oaks Dream*
2) *Oracle's Enigma*
3) *First Oracular Oak*
4) *Oracle Oak's Diviner*
5) *Rebooting Oracular Oak*
6) *Rebooting Melchizadek*
7) *Oracular Oak Husbandry*

Ars Ironica Corona {12} *(71-77)*
1) *Moral Combat*
2) *Ars Ironica*
3) *Encyclopedic Britannica*
4) *Embracing New Knowledge*
5) *Clearing the Canon*
6) *Physical Metaphysics*
7) *Recycled Books*

Angel Trumpets {13} *(85-91)*
1) *All for your Everything*
2) *Time Heals and Wounds to Heal*
3) *Spirit Guide*
4) *Incarnadine Mind*
5) *Divined Family*
6) *Great Catch*
7) *Body's Heir*

Under the Orbital Lilac Tree

IV. Curvism

Com-Pounded Chinese Shakespeare Shavings

Dust Crowned Quintessence {14} *(92-98)*
1) *Jot and Titillate*
2) *When God Particles Collide*
3) *Einstein's Curvism*
4) *Hamlet's Dust*
5) *Mystery Guessing*
6) *Flash Life*
7) *Mirror Crown*

E=MC Crowned {15} *(99-105)*

Crop Circle Chronicles {16} *(106-112)*

Corona Poetica: Curvism {17} *(113-119)*

Byzantium's Renovation

A Unified Field Ballad

V. Orpheum's New World

Overture*: Visions of Vivian*

Libretto:

Apollo's Muses: Act 1 {18} *(120-126)*
1) *Sonnet Rings*
2) *Relentless Wonder*
3) *Harvest Feast*
4) *Following Apollo*
5) *Supernatural Bridge*
6) *Symphonic Spheres*
7) *Summer Rings*

Orpheus Transformed: Act 2 {19} *(127-133)*
1) *Oracular Oak*
2) *Musical Temple*
3) *Ethereal Wind*
4) *Disappearing Here*
5) *Godhead Grapes*
6) *Nightly Count*
7) *Her New Name*

Orpheum's Reunion: Act 3 {20} *(134-140)*

    8) Shadowed Lyre
    9) Orpheus Recomposed
    10) Orphic Quest
    11) Unearthly Light
    12) Intricate Time
    13) New Dawn
    14) Orpheum & Vivian
    15) Orpheum's Garland
    Finale*: Orpheum's Transformed Vision of Vivian*

Epilogue

Accounting with Cubits: The United States of Arcadia *(148)*
Resurrection Epiphany Crown: Ars Poetica (2015) {22} *(149-151)*
Haunted Generation: Dreaming Truth (2016) *(152)*
Unfinished Bible: Sonnet/Psalm-ets Crown {21} *(141-147)*

    1.) Encyclopedic Run
    2.) Song of Worthiness
    3.) Fermenting Firmament
    4.) Temple Trumpets
    5.) Ancestral Mines
    6.) Reconstitution
    7.) Continental Bride

Ancestral Aliens *(153)*

England's Wandering Haunted Galleon *(154)*

American Eclipse (2017)

    *{ } on the right, crowns numbered {1} through {22}
        followed by 4 epilogue sonnets w/ allusions*

    ( ) Shakespeare Sonnet numbers for allusions *(in italics)*
      -continues through other vols.

    Appendix 1 Forming the Trilogy
            2 Shakespeare's Operatic Sonnets
            3 The New AI Consciousness
    Afterword
    Epithalamic Epilogue & Epitaph

Prints

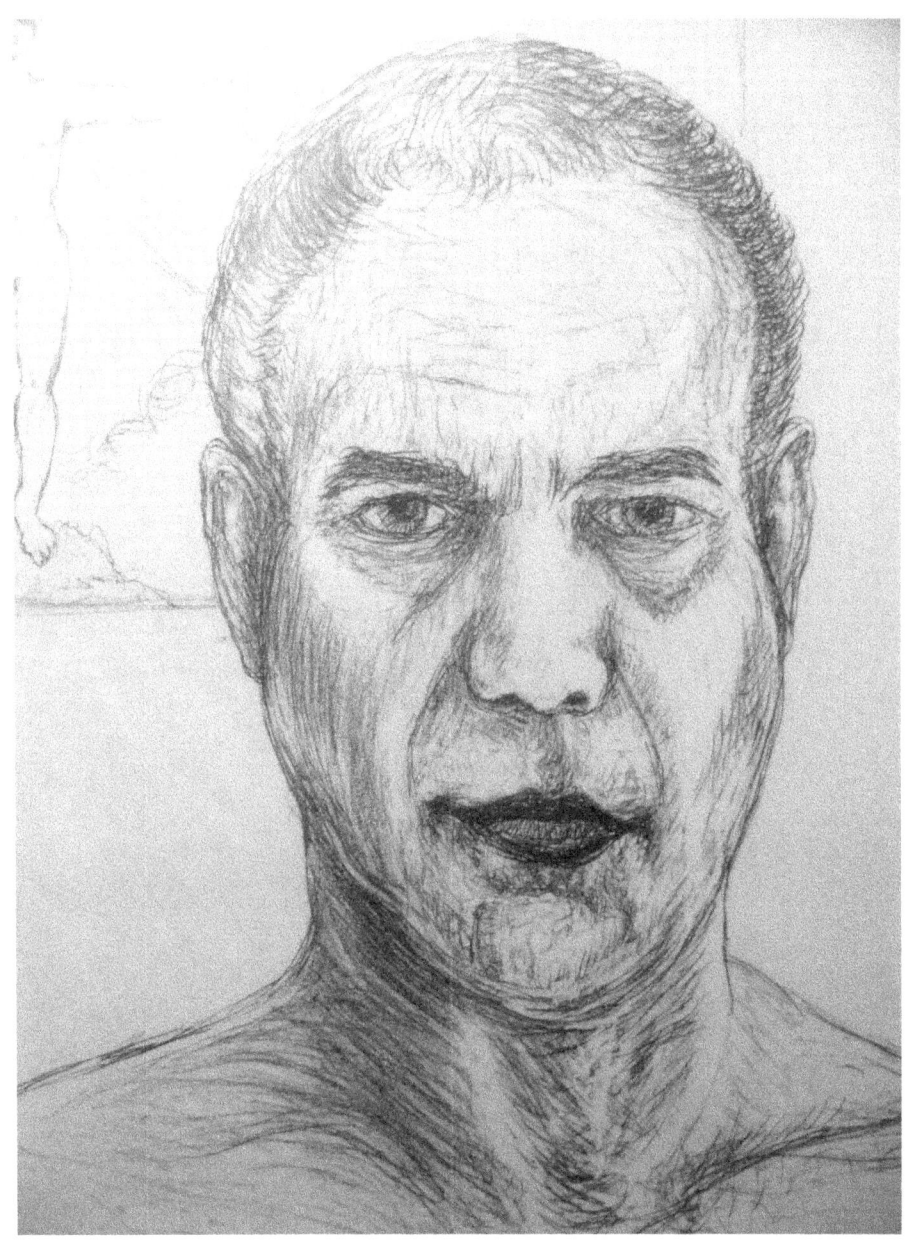

Shakespeare's Wake Reconstructed

Shakespeare AI³, Vol.1

The golden foot I may not kiss or clutch
Glowed in the shadow of the bed
Perhaps it does not come to very much
This thought this ghost this pendulum in the head
Swinging from life to death
Bleeding between two lives
     Awaiting that touch.

The wind sprang up and broke the bells,
Is it a dream or something else
When the sacrifice of the blackened river
Is a face that sweats with tears?
I saw across the alien river
The campfire shake the spears.

　　–T. S. Eliot, *Song to the Opherian*

Visionary Angelic Visitation (2011)

Once dozing lightly
on a poem for Vivian
over thirty years gone,
To Helgoland and Back,
before I'd float
her sonnets on a page,
crown her gravestone.
Night's bed in dark,
outside lit window edge,
sleeping?
A stirring in shadows
darker at foot of bed,
slow seated moves
in hung clothes,
draped chair, turning head,
a moment's doze
fixated angelic being?
My fearless awe saw
cloak hooded face
grow brighter
into her spectral beauty
up lifted bliss face,
brighter inner full moonlight,
looked down, turned cloaked reader,
then writer-reach grasp-moved
my left wrist to chest space,
gave my will written gesture,
bless-checked terror,
vanished as I lurched full-eye-grasp
awakened fear
to circumnavigate a startled
challenged heart.
Night's agon
as unknown what part
of dream's part,
a face's great beauty shone
immortal moon,
from greeting peak joy
to all's well seen,
see you… soon.

Behold, thou desirest truth in the inward parts,
and in the hidden part thou shalt make me to know wisdom.
–Psalm 51
To the chief musician, a Psalm of David (1611, King James Bible

...our little life is rounded
with a sleep...
...to sleep, perchance to dream...
what dreams may come...

–Shakespeare (Hamlet's Tempest)

I Awake

Vivian

Panama Canal Zone, 1974

Barkhausen, Germany,1968

33

Music for Vivian (1995)

When my friend's call turned
to mention her death,
to bare my exclamation
emptied voice,
I begged his pardon,
followed up lost breath,
her graceful passion
rediscovered choice.
Twelve hours bereaved
strums on 12-string guitar,
entwining notes bled
through fingering
flailed hands,
to touch the thought
of her lopsided lost scar
built up crescendos
to long repeated ends.
String broken bell tones,
steel-stinging hollow strains,
communication raptured
fingertips,
wordless conversation
soul attains,
music meditations
on love and friendships.
Now catgut murmurs
her serenity,
the mellow tones,
strong sensitivity.

La Belle Orleanna of the Swamplands {1}

1   *(1)*

Improvisational
cruel
gaudy
fed
tender
heralds, increased
riper creatures,
foes;
rose
due to *famine*
fueled memories
flamed
of *fairest*
ornamental spring,
pity desired
beauties.

2   *(2)*

Archaic *beauties,*
sinking
treasure,
warm
all-eating shamed,
entrenched
deserving a *tattered field,*
gazed briefly,
answers,
twin *haloes,*
*thrifty succession*s.

3   *(3)*

Succession *tombs*
time
fond
April
of her prime,
calls mother's
golden
remembered
age,
hourglass
disdained,
wrinkled husbandry
beguiled.

4   (4)

Beguiled *legacy,*
free largess,
Napoleon
lends
traffic,
a sum of sums,
nature's executors
profit entombed,
leaves bountiful
spent
deceived calls
gone to
nature.

5   (5)

Alligators *still,*
winter
gone
liquid
confounded gentle lease,
distills
hour's lusty
summer
time,
meets
prisoners
never-resting
glass eyed beauty.

6   *(6)*

Beauties of
sweet summer treasured
time,
forbidden,
reconfigured
paid usury
ten times the *willing times*
for *ragged wills loaned*
in *winter,*
conquest posterity,
hands on *vials,*
treasure
distilled.

Pilgrimage
defaced,
mortal golden
high-pitched,
*reeled-*in
steeped
adoring duty,
burning
weary
summer's
converted
youth
ways.

New Orleans Deluge 2005

Vivian's Bremerhaven Crown {2}

1 (1970) **Helgoland** (8)

Hearing the sea,
with
struck ears
tuned
no *war*
reunion,
received
gladly
served
pleasing
sweet concord
single
delight
offended.

2 (1995) **Reunion** (9)

A friend's call
shaped,
enjoyed
shifted
single life
privately
consumed,
hapless
bosoms,
thriftless,
saw
beautiful
fearlessness
issued.

3 (1995) **Countenance** (10)

Bearing evident
beloved-possessed
presence
against
fairness,
gracious providence
proves
beauty conspires
lodged
desiring chiefly
kind-hearted,
repaired
proven.

4 (1970) **Rampant Mothers** (11)

Departure's
fresh blood
minded,
stored
nature's
folly, barren
copied,
sealed
endowed gift
minded,
ceased
featured
lies
shed
rude.

5 (1970) **Impossible Love** (12)

Bristly
counts curled
barren,
to *gird up*
wasted
time,
hideous questions
night-primed,
herd
born
to *beauty's*
defense,
forsaken
silvered over
brave days,
time scythed,
green.

6 (1977) **Janie Lespier** (13)

Leased lovers
semblance
of *issued*
love,
determination
honored husbandry.
Love's
fair
found
upheld
beauty,

formed sweet
dear,
decayed
ending's
eternal
born
storm.

7 (2012) **Visitation?** (14)

Judgment
tells
ends derived,
heaven's
pointing,
good
and evil
constant
season's
fortune,
converts
to read
such art,
predicts
what's plucked,
to thrive
tells.

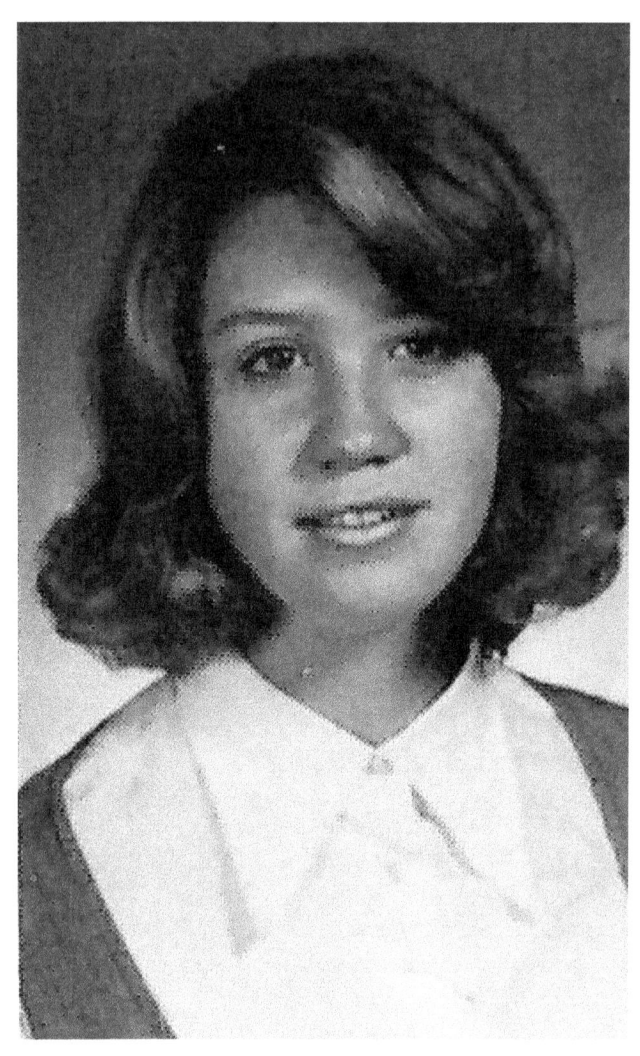

Vivian Moncrief

The Dark Lady's Crown {3}

1 Drawn Shadows   (15)

Check
starry
secret
influenced
brave states
perceived,
stayed
constant,
youth's sap,
rich engrafted,
staged
memory
decayed,
wasted
conceits
war
timed.

2 Dark Lady   (16)

Time's
drawn
maiden garden,
flowers
virtue
wishes,
mighty
eyed
Time's pencil.

Bear my pupil
pen's inner
counterfeit,
happy
painted
unset,
fortified
blessing
repairs,
rhymed
barren
shade.

3 Renovation Lady   (17)

Age
hides,
fills
high
half life
parts
that *touch*
heavenly,
mitered
twice,
yellow paper
truth,
antique
child,
eye
stretched rhymes
true
poets
time.

4 Long Haul   (18)

Days,
shaken in *dim*
wind,
a *summer's*
rough
time
to *shade*
fair
darling
lines
short,
eternal
dated
heaven's
lease
untrimmed,
timed possessions,
temperate nature
wandered,
bragging
faded.

5 Cleft Cleaves   (19)

Faded
lion's
blunt
versed fleeting
fierce
seasonal
devouring,
long-lived
phoenix,

swift-footed
love
hours,
wide
sweet brooding,
untainted
succeeding
pens
in *beauty,*
bleeds,
fades
line's
course.

6 Beginning Ends Again   (20)

Nature's
face
gilded,
passionately
acquainted
love amazes,
changes,
rolls
first
defeated
stolen eyes
on
nothing
of
gentle purpose
at *hand,*
love's heaven.

Susan Austell

7 Masterpiece   (21)

Heaven
rehearsed self love,
painted verse
ornate,
couples'
rondure
heaven,
gold
candle
wind
painted praise,
the *muse's*
first airborne
April,
sold
sea rich gems,
earth ties,
fair sun and moon
love.

There All Along {4}

1   (22)

There
youth again
is given
to presume,
covered
to persuade
in tender
long
time's furrowed days,
expiate
older
looking bearings

2   (23)

Presaged
parts,
imperfect
burdened rite,
tongue forgotten
eloquence,
decayed,
upstaged
fierce recompense,
pleads
to hear
with eyes
love stronger.

3   (24)

Play
painted pride,
painters framed
perspective
skills,
art
held,
truly
drawn
eyes,
windows
eyed
on *tables*
of *recompense*
delights
in *beauty's*
cunning.

4   (25)

Pride,
entitled
favorite honor,
leaves
to *cover joyous*
marigolds,
spread stars,
victories
of a *thousand books*
razed
as *honored,*
famous
toil.

5   (26)

Hope
dares
duty's
great
witness,
bares
gracious
naked
apparel,
appoints
ambassages
of *tattered*
fair aspect
conceits,

6   (27)

Weary
work
abides
on *journey*
of *pilgrimage*
insights,
soul
quiet,
dearly
headed
to *new*
imagination's
travels
of *jeweled*
toil.

Toiled
plight,
bright
gilded,
grief or *graced*
sparkling stars,
consents
flattered
rest,
complexion
brightened,
torture's
pain
& sorrow
resting.

A Considerable Designer Poem

I came upon a monarch
butterfly,
large back trembled
spread out
on parking asphalt,
from poetry's liberal arts
graduate vault
with metrics beaten,
stressed coined words to fly.
The frosty poems
some moth designers spurn
remained in mind
as we slipped through
the door and stepped
our rhythmic feet
up from the floor
out to cocoon cars
where our lines return
to silken webs
if they get spun enough,
pulsed gently like this one
flaps at my feet.
As nature's gift
immediate, complete
to touch, I reached
as then delighted of
and turning over
its wings free to greet,
found a dragonfly
cross-stretched
consuming its treat!
The butterfly's soft beat
flapped to accept
a dragon's culinary need,
flight's due respect.

A Family Man's Thorny Crown {5}

1 Word Sandwich   (36)

Remain
undivided,
love
the *loved*
confessed,
love to *love*
delightful
love effects,
hours
in
public,
stealth
to *wail*
blots
altered,
a*cknowledge*
honors evermore,

2 Sentence   (37)

Crowned
active
abundance,
engrafts comfort
entitled,
wealth despised
wit,
stored
fortune's truth,
lame
shadowed
substance,
a *part's*
sufficed deeds
of *father-fortuned love.*

3 Stand (38)

Verses
of *tenth*
inventions
on *paper,*
rhymes
invocate
perusal
arguments,
vulgar
rehearsals
for *outlived light*
written
worth,
poured
ten times
as *musing breath*
invents,
calls up *nine muses*
to *eternal numbered*
stands.

4 Teacher   (39)

Named
love manners
of *singing*
praises,
divides sweet & sour
worthy proven
leisure,
in *twain*
separates
to *leave*
deceived
torments,
absence
lost suspense,
deserves
love's singular
entertained
watching,
parts time,
teaches
art.

5 Teaching   (40)

Truer
thief
of *love,*
poor love's
grief
receives,
gentle
where *love's*
blame
loves
stealing
love
and *love*
that *loves*
forgives
injured
Love's
graced
will.

6 Paradox (41)

Committed
beauty assailed,
strayed
beauty's
riot
of *art's*
temptation,
beauty
befits
what *beauty leaves*
as *twofold*
when *woman chides*
her *son,*
for *woman's*
pretty wrongs won,
liberty
of *beauty's force*
therefore
prevails.

7 Love   (42)

Love's
joyful
flattery
offense
crosses
dearly
grieving,
touches
nearly,
love
approved,
loved
loves
the *love* of *Love*
Love
suffers.

Zimmerman Madonna

II Un-lost

"No longer wait
 for what I do or say.
 Your judgment now is free
 and whole and true;
 to fail to follow its will
 would be to stray.
 Lord of yourself
 I crown and miter you."

 –Dante, Purgatorio, canto 27, 134-42
   (Anthony Esolen translation)

Orpheus Rising

Dante's Lost Book: Limbo

In exile Dante's vision-damned
enemies, wailed pyro-rhythmic
proto-catechistic views,
pale Virgil's conscience pitied
spiral Roman eyes,
spirit guided circles,
his terror's past reviews,
skewed track,
Deus ex Messiah,
pre-aged pagan wombs,
unbaptized cells,
eternal flame captive bubble,
purgatory's floral hills,
near nine downward dooms,
interment toil,
nature's slave,
cathedral rubble.
Dante's verbal space,
subterranean hollow,
with treadmill quagmires
for the undeveloped soul,
though parchment Sheol
made limbo fallow,
his reservation served
purgatory's bookend role.
Hell's harrowing freed Moses,
Death-Christ retrieval,
as Aaron heard Adam's curse
cured believable.
Great poet shades welcomed
Dante's trapped Virgil strains,
blessed Beatrice
not to read
his lost book in chains.

Inferno Sancti {6}

1 Inferno Sancti   (50)

Sharp
provoked
thrust
weighted
answers,
travel
wretched
to *measure reposed,*
spurs heavily,
seeks
a *journey instinct's*
beastly
groaning speed.

2 Simonized Church (51)

Sped haste
posted
excused
extremities,
new
desired winged-horses
to *neigh*
fiery
perfection's
willfully
poor
slow
spurred
excused
flesh-justice,
dull
mounted
& swift.

3 Bishop's Endgame (52)

Crossing
locked-up
with *seven keys*
pointed
to a *captained*
coming
new
surveyed, proud
imprisoned,
blunting
pleasure riches.
Blessed
solemn
jeweled,
special treasures,
the *wardrobe*
worthy of
an *instant chief*
triumph
of s*et rare stones.*

4 Last Unleavened Way (53)

Bounty substance
lends
shadowed millions
to *tend*
strange
imitations
Adonis can't *describe,*
counterfeits
beauty to
art,

68

a Grecian spring
harvest
renews.
shows one
speaks
to external
shade,
a heart's
tended grace
shaped beauty
blessed,
constantly.

5 Priceless Inheritance (54)

Lovely summer's
rose
buds
perfumed
tinctured virtue,
ornaments
respected
blooms
hung
on thorns,
sweet death,
odors of untruth
disclosed truthful canker
in deep dyes,
breath distilled
fairer
pervading beauty
versed.

6 Rabbi's Beloved Companion's Trust   (55)

End
swept up,
fiery quick
burning
still on gilded
living
power,
memory's stone
praised
posterity,
death's
wasteful
war
paced,
overturned
to marbled
oblivious doom,
enmity's
judgment
prince,
raised
sword of Mar's
war monument,
roots out love's
bright masonry.

7 Savvy Grace   (56)

Spirits edge
love
of *tomorrow's*
appetite,
loves
daily
tomorrow's hungered
love
renewed.
Killed wish,
dull afflictions,
returned blessed
cared for
perpetual ocean,
the *interim's*
welcome filling winter
viewed,
said sweet love
contracts
full summer's force,
sees banked sad time
allayed.
Today parts
to shore a rare wink
sharp
& blunt.

Infallible Politics Uncrowned {7}

1 Re-quested Ring Unsealed   (43)

Eyes
on *night*
shadows
direct fair shades
unseen,
respect shadowed
darkened eyes,
darkly bright
shades,
shadows
heavy dream
imperfect sleep to *clear*
sightless eyes of *night*
living day blessed,
dreams
of *shades*
to *shine*
dead eye days.

2 Recycled Encyclicals   (44)

Trans-*substantial*
injurious
space
limits,
where
one *foot stands*
removed,
jumps
as soon as
thought,
of *thought*
leapt miles,
on *watery*
earth

attended
receiving elements,
slow
fleshed.

3 Sequestered Gestations (45)

Fair
health
absent
purged
alone,
assured
present
tender
returns
recur
in *sweet*
melancholy
motions
of *fire's*
messenger
recounting
life's
oppressive
sad
embassy.

4 Catacomb Conclave (46)

Immortal sense,
divides
war
eyed
as
eye's thought
pleads for
freedom's
conquest.
Titles
plead a *verdict's*
pierced crystal,
heart pictured
tenants
of *heart's*
closet.

5 Sexual Taxation of a Holy Stimulus (47)

The *league's*
good turns,
famished,
smothered
painted banquet,
pictures
famished
parts
of the *feast,*
lovers'
delight smothered,
shares
parts
asleep
in *love.*

6 Unsexed Politics (48)

Comforting
trusted
hands
on *trifling*
falsehoods
jeweled
worthy
of *vulgar*
grief's
truest trifles,
lock up
destiny's
thrust
in *wards*
of *artful prey.*

7 Feral Government Tamed (49)

Audits
call love advised,
scarcely
prime time
in *deserts*
timed,
reared up sums,
to *part reason's knowledge,*
guard
ensconced greetings
against law's
that *cast sun*
on *settled gravity,*
passing strange hands
strengthen
to *leave defecting,*
alleges love's
respected
love
eyes
converts.

Democrates Demoed (philosopher's fragment) -after A. Dürer

Crown of Creation {8}

But what thy thorny crowne gain'd, that give mee,
--John Donne

1 Passover   (57)

Time's
=shadowed= *slave*
chided
=God's proof= ,
desired
=mercy's= *fool.*
From =lion's= *ill*
questioned
=fallen= *slaves,*
to *dare* that *sad* =sung= *affair*
=awake=,
to *bid adieu,*
tend to
=nation's=
sovereign
=soul fixed=
bitterness,
precious
=set spear= *spent,*
watched
poured love =pressed=,
world-without-end
hours =laid=,
saved
from =net=
clocked =pit=.

2 Unleavened Days   (58)

Sufferers
of =earth=,
=God's= *slaves*
to =judgment's=
chartered
=deal=,
time's
=wicked=
privilege,
craves
=mischief stopped=.
=Blood= *tamed*
=thorns=
=vexed=,
hell
bound
=footsteps=
imprisoned,
tamed =astray=,
pardoned for =refusing=,
patience =runs= to
=righteous=
sufferance,
liberty's
=fruit=
beckoning pleasure
blamed
=blood=.

3 Pentecost (59)

New
=blood's=
=might=
beguiles
labor's invention,
=sees wicked=
=souls=,
former =God= *child's*
second =strength= to
compose,
the *same backward* =refuge=
till 2 *five hundred courses*
of sun's =perish=,
with *records* =gathered=,
that *frame*
antique book's =consumed=,
new
wonders =abroad=
mended,
Old world's character
=returns= when *done,*
your love's =prepared=
revolution.
The *image*
=rises up= to *better*
minded =mercy lips=
from =scattered=,
former =day's=.

4 Trumpets (60)

=Scattered= *ends*
=shake=
waves toward
the pebbled shore,
delved
scythes
=divide= *all*
in parallels
=strong=.
Crooked-times
=deliver=
nature's ends,
=divides=
cruel handed
=Edom's= *eclipsed* =heavy=
=wash-pot=,
contends with
main =cast out=
lightning
to *transfix*
minutes =leading=
a =deadly= *stand* =down=.
Time's Nativity
=*truth* treads down=,
fights =trouble's=
stand,
crowns
=love's=
=triumph=.

5 Atonement (61)

Love's
=vow=
=prayed=
a *watchman's*
slumbering =ear= *awake,*
to =hear= *great*
=hope=,
=endures=
=God's= *shadow*
deed
=covered=
=year=.
True will =gives=
=generation heritage=
eyes,
=dwells= in
=*desire*=
=given= *love* =trust=,
scopes weary =life=,
=names=
tenor =praised= *home*
=preserved= in *spirit's*
jealous image,
=performs day's mercy=
for *shame* of
=*love*= *elsewhere's*
=heavy= *watch.*

6 Tabernacles (62)

Self-love
=waiting=
=breaks=
=weight= on *remedy*
=*imagined*=
=increase=.
Iniquity's self-love
=falls=
like a =stone=,
on *shapes of* =human=
love inward parts.
Beat =broken slain= *antiquity*,
the =rock's= *possession*
grounds,
=*every soul's* exalted *heart*=
=belongs strengthened=
defines accounting =power=
of *true heart* =souls=,
the *sin painter's* =work=
of *self's truth age*;
=God= surmounted =defense=
praises =trusted=
gracious beauty
=delights=.

7 Last Great Day (63)

Beauty
=magnifies= *away* =all=
travels =worldwide=,
the *hours* =satisfy=
youthful =wings=.

"If =they= =thirst=,
let =flesh= *vanish*
to *spring*
=waters= of *life,*"
the =*King*=
fills
=loving=
=soul= *ages.*

=Those held=
in *cruel*
=sworn=
living,
rise to *love*
=commended= *time,*
now =Creator= *sight,*
treasure =portioned=
lines,
time's wrinkle
=shadowed= *lines.*

Shakespeare Sonnets (57-63); =Coverdale psalms= same
numbered (57-63) allusions; in Shrouded Crown (64-70)

Shrouded Crown {9}

Joseph took the body, and wrapped it
in a clean linen shroud, and laid it in his own
new tomb, which he had hewn in the rock.
–Matt.:27:59/60 (R. S. V.)
God be merciful.. bless us.. shew us the light
of his countenance… –Psalm 67:1 (Coverdale)

1 On the Shroud (64)

=Judge preserved=
time's slave,
=sudden perfect insurrection=
buried, outworn
=wounds=
of *age's*
kingdom,
lofty =wicked=
time's
=bitter=
=heard tongues=,
hands defaced =fallen=,
=deep= *soil*
hungry mortal
ocean of =perceived=
interchanges,
down-razed,
=laid=
state,
loss, firm,
=swift=
to =secret= *shore,*
the *state itself,*
loss =work=,
eternal =love=,
death's gain,
=gathered=
rich cost.

2 Relic Shroud   (65)

=E*arth*=
stone jewels,
=broad=
boundless
miracle gate
=received *rage*=
held plea,
sad stout
=crowned=,
impregnable =folds=,
wracked =salvation=.
What =mad= *hand's*
beauty =blessed=
rock-dust *flowers,*
timed =Jerusalem=?
(Secundo Pia's) =evening=
day's bright ink,
best =morning=
black foot,
=*he* dropped *still*=
to *meditation power,*
=God= *swift*
mortality,
=full furrowed=
=vows= *held*
out.

3 Shrouded Belief   (66)

Leave alone
what =vows *hold*=,
=wealthy= *rest's*
faith,
=worship=
controlled skill,
=who holds
our souls=.
Doctored =work=
nothing trimmed,
=proven= *needy,*
forsworn authority
disgraced,
=inclined= to be
=mis*placed*=,
=offers=
death's
=paid trouble=,
the =exalted=
right cry =honored=,
time's
=suffering=
captive =silver=
twice *tongue-tied*
too =wicked= to
simply =speak=.

Proud =ends=
=all light= *of true days'*
seek plural 's'
=health=,
infected to =show=
=ways=
for =world saving=
lively =mercy=
on *impious* =nations=
=judged=.
Why should false painting
imitate =us righteously=
=among= *sin laced*
=people=
with *advantages for*
who *should achieve*
what =earth brings=
beggars in
its *shadow*?
Why did poor beauty
=increase=,
bankrupt
to *live*,
blush his *blood's*
=known= *rose hue,*
=governed= *presence,*
death =countenance=
grace?

5 Entered Shroud   (68)

=Prepared=
death map
for *sepulcher* =salvation's=
fair art,
day's green
=divided spoil=
stored,
outworn =habitation=,
renewed sign seen
head =inherited=,
a second life
from =perished=
=ridden=
=silver wings=
=scattered=,
=holy=
antique hours
shorn,
=mindful wilderness=,
born bastard
=captive= *nature's*
=gold feather=
=defended fatherless=,
new ornamental
second =earth=,
dressed map
of =cloud=
beauty.

6 Love's Shroud (69)

=E*ye*=
beauty's
thoughts of
=heaven=,
=table= *curled*
measures of
soil =possessions=.
=Salvation= *due*
=covers= =place=
in =soul= *voiced*
deeds
even foes commend.
Bare truths =power=
=living books= *unuttered,*
matching
=multitudes written=,
=drawn=
outward
ranks crowned,
nothing matches
=earth=
flowered
=servant= *praised*
accents,
=given *mercy's*=
outward show
=delivered=
hearts.

7 Stumbling on the Shroud

(70)

=Delivered= *hearts*
of *cankers*
=seek salvation's=
defect =confounded=
from *ornamental kingdom*
=confusion=,
approved suspects
=rewarded=,
good blaming
=*praised*=
=longer= to
show unstained,
heaven's sweetest air flown,
=shamed=
=haste= *tied,*
marked =redeemer=
presented
mask,
=poor=
charges owed
=brought God=
slandered
=shame=
enlarged
=backward turn's=
pure prime
=judged=
times.

III Visitation

Floral Crown {10}

(allusions from Shakespeare's embedded love crown
variation beginning here -to a veritable love garland)

1 Symmetrical Flower   (29)

Scope
sweet
fortune
rebooted hope,
enjoy wealth of
rising wishes
that *break earth*
on a *rich day*
in cursed states.
Eyes on self
sing trouble's hymn
to *deaf heaven,*
king's disgrace,
an *outcast's sullen fate*
scorned thoughts
despised at the *gate,*
contentment changing least,
heaven's larked estate
remembers featured
art
haply loved.

2 Leonardo's Cathedral Pod   (30)

(Love)
summons
to
flow up
from *sessions*
of *remembered*
past things,
friends,
dated nights,
precious
flow,
sad drowned foregone,
cancelled
vanished sight…
accounted death
thought new,
restored
losses,
heavy
on woe-eyes.

3 Blossomed Mind   (31)

*View
all dead,
love's
trophy
tears,
interest hidden
love,
buried
bosoms,
viewless
counterpart
burials,
Love reigns in
love of lovers,
all in All's
image,
holy
Love's
obsequious parts
lacking
(death).*

4 Floral Gift   (32)

Survey
fortune,
time's curved
days
reserved,
for *loved ones*
loving lifts
the *pen,*
the *lovers'* gaze
on *rude lines*
exceed
to o*utstrip*
covers
of *happier deceased poets*
who *rank*
love rhyme
styles
of *love compared*
muses.

5 Spiritual Bridal Bouquet

(33)

Stain
kissed heads,
disdained
world alchemies,
gilded brows,
tributes
a *sovereign*
steals
of *cloud climbed*
glory,
a *mountain-top woman's*
heavenly face,
morning's hidden visage
hours,
triumphant region's
splendor,
heaven sustained
love
world.

6 Floral Rapture   (34)

Love
ransoms,
cloaked
cloudy
smoke
physics,
storm-beaten days,
disgraced
shameful wounds salved,
loss spoken
rain
cures,
bears tears
of repented
ill deeds,
Pearl faced
grief,
great rich relief,
hidden rotten
sorrow-shed,
healed dry offenses
breaking clouds,
love crossed
braver promises.

7 Floral Miracle (35)

Budding
sweet
roses
as *cankers*
corrupt,
sense
thorny faults.
Excusing lawful pleas,
trespassed strains
commence in *fountain mud,*
a *thief's sin*
lives in,
its *advocates,*
love
authorized
civil war,
hate to *grief,*
sensual accessories
to *excuse*
cloudy faults,
compare to
moon
eclipsed
silver light.

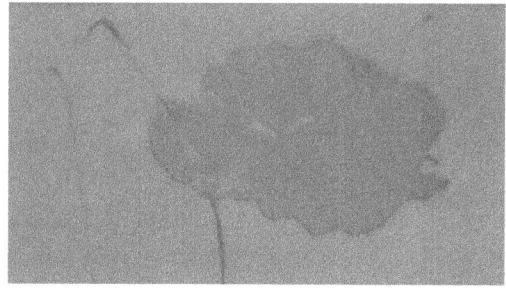

Oracular Oaks {11}

1 Breathing Oaks Dream   (78)

I*nvoke*
heights
these *eyes*
compiled,
proud double majesty
to *muse* on *verse*
dispersed,

eyes
of *art*
in *rooks*
aloft,

alien
pen
taught
feathered wings,

high
(moss)
on (bark) *to sing.*

2 Oracle's Enigma   (79)

Gracious
argued
travails
that *pay* to *reinvent*
poets,
grace stolen word
virtue,
to *place*
with *numbered*
pens
paid
in *love afforded praise,*
calls for aid
(Abe) *mused* on.

3 First Oracular Oak   (80)

T*hrive*
bark
tongues,
building
mighty
spoken fame,
worthy
broad main afloat,
saucy
sailed
pride,
soundless
(Abraham)
tall
cast.

4 Oracle Oak's Diviner   (81)

Breath,
surviving past
memory,
live
name
created,
death-wish
yielded,
rehearsed
tongues,
immortal monument
reading
life.

5 Rebooting the Oracular Oak (82)

Day's
abuse,
time-tainted
gross
enforced,
telling
dedication,
painting
devised rhetoric
hue's
strained knowledge,
subject
booked,
word's
worth fresher
blessings
of past
loves.

6 Rebooting Melchizadek   (83)

Found
modern
barren
reports
impute
debt
devised,
exceed
dumb
entombed,
impaired
slept
fair eyes,
tender penned.

7 Oracular Oak Husbandry   (84)

Penned
cursed copy
alone,
blessed,
admired,
subjects
equal
fame
dignified
dwelling,
stored immured
rich glory,
clear
confined
counterparts
grown
story.

Ars Ironica Corona {12}

1 Moral Combat   (71)

Sullen
warnings
surly
vile
written
world
no remembered
verse
writ
thinking,
warned
world's
compound
rehearsed bells
decayed
wise world
mocked.

2 Ars Ironica   (72)

Task
this
nothing
to *hang* how *death*
forgets,
merits
devised
prove
untrue
virtuous lies,
imparts
truth
shamed
worth,
deserted
well spoken
names
recited,
a *world's*
buried true love,
of *nothing.*

3 Encyclopedic Britannica   (73)

*Time's
late love,
sunsets
sweet sung,
day's
twilight
of youth's
rest
to black night
death-bed,
perceives
a second self
unsealed
west
fires away bare
nourished
consuming
glows.*

4 Embracing New Knowledge   (74)

*Lines
reviewed
of earth
reviewers,
memorials
arrest,
remembered
bail
consecrates,
contented
coward's conquest,
the better part of one
wretched life,
prey of worms
spirit
life*

World strife,
life's
by and by,
all gluttons
will
measure,
food
to *possess*
best
peace,
to *starve*
a *clean*
miser's day
by day filching
wealth's treasures,
steal
pining
for
a *proud*
pleasure
counted
age,
alone
to
pursue.

6 Physical Metaphysics   (76)

Versed
quick barren
variations,
old
compounded strange
word
methods,
frame design
invention's,
time's noted weed
argument.
Birth proceeds
newly spent,
when *spending*
estranges
what's
daily
retold.

7 Recycled Books   (77)

Remind
vacant
memory's
new book's,
a *glass*
grave's
eternity contains
brain
blanks,
dials
wrinkle
imprinted
deliveries,
progressive enrichments
set
&
leaves booked
looks.

Angel Trumpets {13}

1 All for your Everything   (85)

Reserved
tongue-tied
compiled,
precious
muse's
hymns,
a *lettered*
clerk's
pen
polished
hearing,
praises
for *love of your*
(*something's*)
respected
effects.

2 Time Heals, Wounds to Heal   (86)

Proud
bound,
rehearsed
verse entombed
spirit,
mortal
night's
lines,
ghostly
feared
nightly
victor's
sickness
filled
lifeline
matters.

3 Spirit Guide   (87)

Farewell's
charter
granted
riches,
bond,
sleep
determined
knowing
swerves
given dreams,
misprisioned
better judgment,
estimates
knowing's
possessed
waking.

4 Incarnadine Mind   (88)

Disposed
merit's
vantage
double
bending
set
gains,
virtuous
injured
scornful
love-light,
tainted
concealed
parts
lost
in eye of scorn
forsworn.

5 Divined Family   (89)

Forsake
defending
tongue's reasoned
acquaintance,
old love's will
beloved ill
loved ones,
dwelling
in will's
desired
telling
named
forms,
reset
debated
vowed
hating.

6 Great Catch   (90)

Wind-bent
world's
rain loss
across woeful
fortune's
escape
of fortune's
grief left spite,
strains
last nights,
their worst
lingered
conquered
deeds
came down
compared first.

7 Body's Heir   (91)

Some glory
to rest
in adjunct
garments,
a richer
body alone,
wealth
measured
body's force,
general
echoed humors,
proud love
bettered,
higher
pleasured
new-fangled
ill's
all.

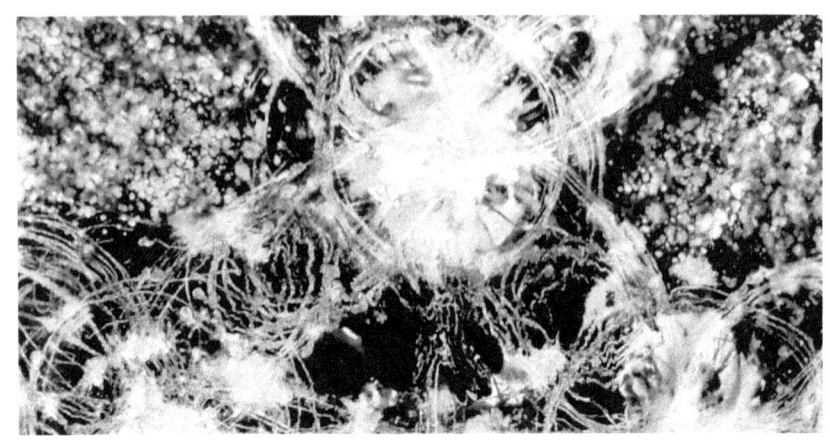

Under the Orbital Lilac Tree

Between the lines' material, chasing the moon
his Kosmos calls from an orbital lilac tree,
as I lie in glowing fields, dream up his night's tune,
its taproot tallying the orbs of destiny.
To watch him gaze at stars, the same wrapt everything,
no old man here from timeless aspirations fled,
his daylight transcendental smile, Kosmic thinking
eclipses earth with other moons where death has sped.
Like night-birds to her virtue's inward sunshine eye,
content perfection's inherited grace
as sudden ease of focus pulls love in to fly,
desire's sweetest lines, curve to her sovereign face.
Why would love happen not at death's call of beauty?
There'll be no "no's" for you to not know no pity.

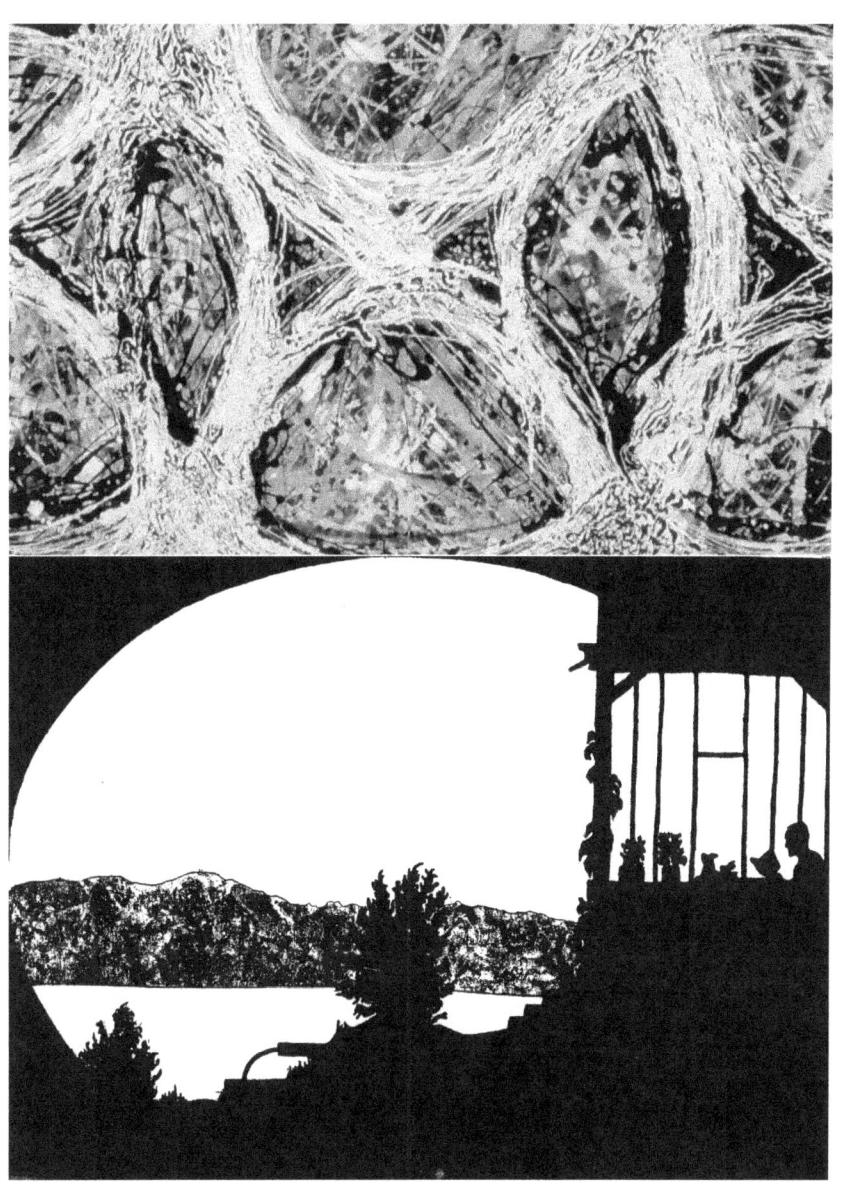

IV *Curvism*

Compounded Chinese Shakespeare Shavings

The magnet's iron filing
steel dust rose,
shaped form as forced,
eyes its own image.
The lines extend
what was common prose,
bent back on its dot matrix
like-minded mirage.
The force through glass
by what's seen new
when shavings move
in joined procession,
vibrate pixel strands,
prove ultra blue.
A vision shape
curved contact connection,
billions of years pulse
time's spinning atoms,
lined filings up to fill
from light force spent
on what keeps a force field
curving into blooms
gravity imposes
sunlight to be bent.
The shavings on this page
have claimed the space
eyes crawl from line
to mind gravitating in place:
Pound loved oriental forms
steel filings made
as young Einstein's magnetized
compass needle played.

Dust Crowned Quintessence {14}

1 Jot and Titillate   (92)

Love
assured
longer
than
inconstant
worst
wrongs,
least
dependent
better
entitled mind,
vexed
revolting humor,
terms to *find,*
happy to *die* for
life's
(curved) *nature.*

2 When God Particles Collide   (93)

He*aven's*
new altered
serving
answer,
looks on
change's
historic
wrinkle,
Eve's apple,
dwells
in *placed*
works,
telling
of *grown,*
eyed artful
creations.

3 Einstein's Curvism   (94)

Turn
things far,
unmoved by
nature's riches,
of *stones expense,*
slow to *itself*
facing
deed
inherited
graces,
summer's cold
sweet moves
(curved) to
dignified stars.

4 Hamlet's Dust (Heroic)   (95)

Dost
the *lovely story*
sport sin,
dispraised,
lascivious
fragrant shame?
Comments
ill-used,
the *reporter's*
privilege,
naming
habitation
cankers,
uncovered blots,
enclosed
veiled vices,
eyeing
knives on
dear budding names,

day's
blotted beauty,
a wanton turn,
covered
blessed
disgraces.

5 Mystery Guessing   (96)

D*isgraces*
grace youth
of *gentle sport,*
base faults
jewel
esteemed
fingering
on a *queen's*
sterner truth,
translations
truer errors,
translated strength
stated,
betrayer's
less throned
faults.

6 Flash Life   (97)

Winter's
dark days,
freezings,
pleasure's fleeting
barest
time removed,
autumn's timing,
summer's burden,
primed to *bear*
abundant fruit
issues
from increased
teeming
orphan wombs,
hope's pleasures
cheered
my mute bird
absent
winter
unfathered dull.

7 Mirror Crown   (98)

Winter absent
April,
spring bird laughter,
plucks pride
leaping,
to *make*
wonder,
summer spirits
deep,
heavy Saturn
stories.
Patterned
different youth
tell of *their*
hue drawn
flower figured
trims,
rose shadow's
dressed
(curve).

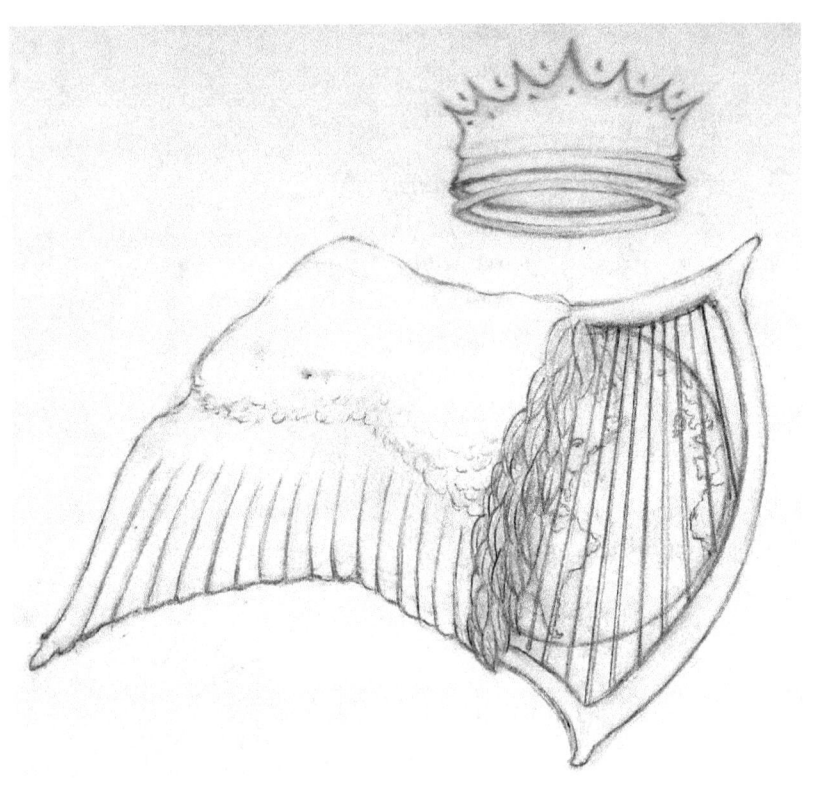

E = MC Crowned {15

1   (99)

One
stolen,
death
condemned,
dwells on
stealing
sweet
color's
forward,
gross growth
dyed
ultraviolet,
fearful flowering
pride's
canker.

2   (100)

Mused
dark famed
art power
numerically
redeemed
spends
decay's
fury
of *crooked*
pens,
time's
straightened
wrinkle
based
skill,
might
argue
to *rise*
with the *muse.*

3　　(101)

Muse
on muse
fixed
gilded lies,
laid
entombed
to *outlive truths,*
to *teach intermixed,*
pencil
truth
answered
ages
now.

4　　(102)

Now
delight
as *mournful*
pipes
esteem
hymns
of summer
nights,
love
riper
wild music,
new songs
rich commonly
sung
in *uncommon*
tongues.

5 LIGO's Gravity Dance Soundtrack   (103)

Versed
muse
adds
more worth,
mends
blunt pride,
bare
arguments,
invention's
scoped
subject
glass,
strives
faced
with grace.

6   (104)

The old-eyed
dial-hand,
stands
processes
perceived,
fresh as
spring perfume,
turns seasonal
motions reborn,
cold hues burnt,
first figures
deceiving heat,
beautifully perceived
beauties.

7 Einstein's Curvism II   (105)

Love's
three themes in one,
shows
kind wondrous
ones,
today's invented idol
confines,
to *love*
fair constant
ones in
tomorrow's songs,
love's true
beloved
verse
varied
scope,
spent
constancy,
ones change
(curve)
expressed
as
one.

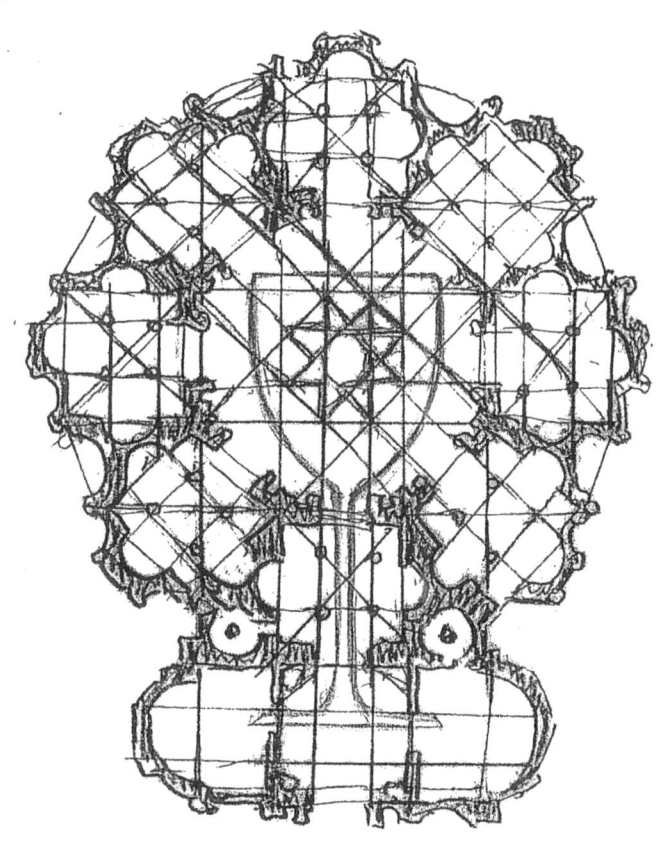

Crop Circle Chronicles {16}

1   (106)

Chronicles
of *antique days,*
hand, foot, lip,
brow
prefigured
time
mastered
blazoned
rhymed,
divining
worth,
knight's
timed
present
prophecy
pens of now.

2   (107)

Prophetic
souls'
presaged.
control,
confines
augured
moon eclipse
assured,
rhymed in *tribal*
over dull
monuments,
a *crown's endless*
weave
speechless,
subscribed
to *proclaim*
endurance
time's
peace.

3 (108)

Love
of *time's*
divine
loves
register
antiquity's
expressed
wrinkles,
figures
brain
spirit
merits,
an *age's*
e*ternal*
new.

4 (109)

Universe
traveled,
stained
range
reigned-in,
(Carl Sagan's '74)
nature wide
time
exchanged,
all souls called
from false
to *time's*
good
summing
home.

5   (110)

Old
gone
there ends here,
grinds
true
(Wiltshire hillside)
confined
looks,
proof,
essays
proved
truth
viewed
thoughts
of *gods.*

6   (111)

Potions
fortune
godhead
deeds,
the *brand's*
hand
works
the *hand's*
public
manners,
drinks in
friend's
bitter work's
dyer
doubles.

7 (112)

World
stamped,
all-the-world's
thrown
steel
dispensed
sense,
dead
bred
in *vulgar*
scandal
tongue's
abyss
marking
(Stonehenge curves).

Leonardo's First Picnic

Corona Poetica: Curvism {17}

"When man wanted to make a machine that would walk he invented
the wheel, which looked nothing like a leg. In doing so he was practicing
surrealism without knowing it."
–G. Apollinaire (inventor of the words "cubist" and "surreal")

1   (113)

Shapes
govern
a *mind's*
function,
birds
to *outbound*
sea objects,
forms
catch a *mountain's*
true
features.
Complete
night mind,
incapable of
ocean
delivered day effect's
gentle
sweet favors
parting
quick eye's blind sight,
holds vision's
mind
shaped
heart.

2　　(114)

First crowns
beam up
a monster's
fast
mind's-eye
true to sight,
best
(curves) *perfect*
as alchemy creates,
cherubim being
assemblages
greeted
with monarch objects,
kingly-taught
mind-eye
prepared
great cupped love
agreeing palates,
less poison
drunk
of indigestible
plagued
creatures.

3   (115)

As lines grow
reckoning
full time
vow's,
sharper
intents,
diverted afterwards,
strong beauty
crowned decrees,
blunt uncertainties
in time's
course,
changes
to love's
judgment,
the million-reasons-love
flamed creeps through
a rested mind,
written
why accidental
altered
love
fears.

4　　(116)

True mind's written
marriage
bears fixed tempests
taken on love's
alteration
&
starry wandering barks,
their *worth ever*
comes out
to *love's look*,
removes doom
of *bending sickle's*
rosy cheeked
lips
love altered,
encompassed hours and weeks,
brief shaken
love time
fool-proof
altered,
bending edges
to *unknown heights*.

5   (117)

All transport's
bond,
wind's frequent (curve),
repays hate's
errors,
hoists sail tied
mind in *surmise*
of a*ll*
Time
surmised,
just proof
accumulated,
accused day's leveled
unknown
love
to *prove*
further willfulness
in *scant books*
constancy,
love's (trilogy)
awakens
the call's
appealed
virtues
all-within.

6 (118)

Appetite's compound
purge,
sickness curved
& illness
urged
to *shun*
disease.
Loves
prevention policy
states full
framed malady's
goodness
faults.
Keen bitter sauces
fed the *drug's*
ill lessons,
cure's
poisonous
ranked
true medicine,
assures
eager
anticipated
welfare
found.

7   (119)

Siren
fears
of *hell*
hopes
that
hope's
fair
great spheres
rebuke
wretched
new evil.
Better built
lost
alembics spent
fever fitted
first committed
error's,
gained
ill mad
distractions:
content
fears
of far
applied benefits,
ill
distilled
love's
still
(curve).

Byzantium's Renovation

The artifice
of ageless computations
transmuted gold's timeless
goldsmith matters,
Jerusalem walls
with new equations,
set tower code,
ancient angel ciphers
on wings of state
blueprint liberty slates;
arcane song improvised
new wherewithalls,
dominion's memory
for later dates,
what's yet to come
recorded in the halls.
Iconic power's future
spiral cycles
to generate new
current golden oracles,
star field symmetry,
argus angel morphosis
sifts qubit wall derived
dimension calculus,
a Delphic voice
on Apollonian reason,
the Way's new name
singing on a white stone.
No human hand hews
its measured season,
celestial light-beamed
hybrid renovation.

A Unified Field Ballad

To touch fingers
of nature's hidden hand
and tally out
numerological laws,
warp & weft
of sky related to land
the way ground gravitates
in space-time's pause.
Why does the hydrogen
atom not radiate
like Mercury spinning
around the sun,
as geometry's warps
& curves calculate
an ever accelerating
creation?
The black hole center
turned against curvature
within blackout moonstone's
sarcophagus roll,
stone tossed ripple's
mathematical architecture
shows consciousness
where time lapsed
a slower hole,
the great equation's
AI unification,
eternity's past,
future now
timed unison…

V *Orpheum's New World*

Overture: Visions of Vivian

When Orpheus tuned
the lyre to his muse
searching for a way
to sing Eurydice
another life without
a third to lose,
seed notes vined phrases
melodiously.
Twined strings bent
their melancholy zenith,
incited forest wildlife
lulled in peace,
nine muses inspired
by supreme Tenth
till jealous Maenads severed
his six string sense.
Death vortex dreams
morphed him to Orpheum,
there, found Vivian,
transposed in name.
Tuned as Apollo's son
he composed
improvisational love
in tandem
rose to intuitive love
in unison with Vivian
in the vale of heaven.
Twice dying,
transformed Eurydice's pain,
his once to variations,
next to her terrain,
transposed in earth's core
to celestial refrain,
Vivian's double love
in the vale of heaven.

Apollo's Muses (Act 1) {18}

Muse of my native land! Loftiest Muse!
Rapt in deep prophetic solitude…
There came an eastern voice of solemn mood:
Then sang forth the nine, Apollo's Garland–
–Keats, Endymion, IV

1 Sonnet Rings   (120)

Time's
10th Muse *tenders*
sorrow,
wounds
true
hell,
ransomed
steel time
befriended trespass,
crime
passed
remembered
ransom
shaken,
hammering
hardened
leisure taken,
transgressions
tyrants suffer,
bowed sorrow
weighed.

2 Relentless Wonder   (121)

Count
esteemed
pleasures,
will's
I Am as I Am
spied,
rendered,
maintained,
beveled
vile,
sportive
better
ranking deeds,
salutation
levels
the *reign's*
(wonder).

3 Harvest Feast   (122)

Bolder
memory's
dated
nature
razed
tables.
score
idle
missed
flights,
retention
records,
oblivion
tallied gifts
table
eternity.

4 Following Apollo   (123)

True
built
born
novel
desires
wondering,
defying
passed
Orpheus
in *present*
Apollo
dressed
best
haste
recorded
register
vows.

5 Supernatural Bridge   (124)

(Apollo's)
call
times stated
weeds & flowers,
builds
subjected fortune,
blown
numbered
policies,
invites
no fear,
leases
time
fashioned
(Orpheus)
to witness
(muses)
times.

6 Symphonic Spheres   (125)

(Apollo's)
based
dwelling's
outward gaze
compounds
canopy
controlling
honors,
informing
eternity's
favored
(symphonic)
seconds
savoring
impeached
obsequious
souls.

7 Summer Rings   (126)

Sovereign
power (rings)
(summer)
lover's
onward
mistress
nature,
withering
purpose
pleasures
grown,
keeps time
detained
minion's
waning,
plucked
fickle
lovely
times.

Orpheus Transformed (Act 2) {19}

In immeasurable darkness, empowering...
if the earthly no longer knows your name,
whisper to the silent earth: I'm flowing...
to the flashing water say: I am.
 –Rilke, *Sonnets to Orpheus*, II, 29

1 Oracular Oak   (127)

Beauty's
counted
name,
successive
power
slandered
bastard
beauty,
borrows
nature's
bower,
empowered
profane
mournful
holy old
beauty's
brow,
beauty's
disgraced
raven's
sweet
tongue.

2 Musical Temple   (128)

The *ear* s
concord
(Eurydice)
musical
fingered
happy
nimble
lips,
dancing
wood,
swayed
inward leaps.
(Apollo's)
hand
motions
harvest stands
(to the 10th Muse)
gentle
living lips,
blessed kiss
of
wood.

3 Ethereal Wind   (129)

Possession's
bliss
spirits
reason's
quest,
all this
world's proof,
sky-*proven*
Apollo,
extreme
savaged
(Delphic)
purpose
pursuits,
extreme
joy,
heaven's
dream
bliss
hunt
proposed,
straight
from
trusting
woe's
madness.

4 Disappearing Here   (130)

Goddess
of *violet*
sun's
wired
rose
cheeks,
love
breathless
as *her*
grew to *speak,*
heard love's
mistress,
(to Orpheus)
she'd walk
her black
rare wired
underground music,
tread
ground
sounds to *nothing.*

5 Godhead Grapes   (131)

Nothing dearer
groaning
heart,
judgment's
faith,
beauty's
thousand
precious
fairest
proud
proceeds,
(Eurydice's)
artful
slandered
(East Elysian)
witness.

6 Nightly Count   (132)

East
disdained,
mourned, pitied
mourning,
Pluto's *pain*
tormented glory,
graced sober,
love ushered
mournful
even star,
to *mourn*
(nightly) *morning*
mourns
(orphic) *pity,*
swears her
(new Vivian)
heart's,
in *heaven.*

7 Her New Name   (133)

Vivian's *heart*
for Orpheus
groaned
tortured,
forsaken,
enslaved,
prison
crossed
torments.
(Maenads)
bailed his *taken*
wounds engrossed
(muses)
de-*rigor*-ed
his *guard,*
deep pent in
ward of
(Orpheum's)
force.

158

Orpheum's Reunion (Act 3) {20}

Orpheus with his lute made trees,
And the mountain tops that freeze,
Bow themselves when he did sing...
  –Shakespeare, *Henry VIII*, 3.1.35

8 Shadowed Lyre   (134)

(Apollo's) *will*
when (Maenads)
mortgaged
(Orpheus),
their *covetousness*
restored
forfeited
his *loss*.
(Vivian's) *still*
willed
surety
freed
to *bind*
bonds,
indebted
her
beauty
paid whole
will to
(Apollo's)
will.

9 Orpheus Recomposed   (135)

(Apollo's)
will-wished
added
will's
will to *vex*
will's
made-over shine,
wills
booted
spacious
under-*will*-tones.
(Orphic) *will's*
willing
sea will
vouched as
water will's
riches,
willed
beseeched
abundance
will as (Orpheum's)
& (Vivian's) *will,*
a *kind*
sweet Orphic
still-will.

10 Orphic Quest   (136)

Sweet (Orphic)
still-willed
will fulfilling
(Elysian Fields)
reckoned
love-suited
full
filled
will
reproved
treasured will,
numberless
accounts,
untold
sweet receipts,
will stored
nothing's
with filled
love's
blind will.

11 Unearthly Light   (137)

When *blind*
false corrupt
partial
forged beauty
of *falsehood's*
plot ridden lies,
fouls
the *best* as *worst,*
transfers
fool hearted
plagued
judgments,
several
hook-eyed
wide world bays
see commonplace
truth
anchored.

12 Intricate Time   (138)

Truth
suppressed,
when sworn
untutored subtleties
believe the *best,*
vain
love
simply
from a *day's*
fault
is not false.
(Orpheum's)
simple
world
of *young love's*
habitat
(Vivian) *trusts*
old love
age's
known.

13 New Dawn   (139)

Known
art's
heart wounded
powers,
elsewhere's
cunning
calls
overpressed,
faces
injuries with
elsewhere's
lovely
turn
on (Vivian)
& (Pegasus)
defensive
tongue.

163

Tongue
pressed
patience
better
to disdain
as Maenad-*slandered*
world
madness,
their *pity-wanting pain*
in word
despaired,
physician
mad
ill-resting words,
(Maenad)
sick expressed
(Orpheus) *sorrows.*
Proud (Vivian's)
wit mannered
wisdom grows
(oak) *health*
to (lyre)
teacher.

15 Orpheum 's Garland

As beauty's lyre cut
teacher counted branches,
the ear shaped tongue's
eponymous temple
possession of the root
wood's branched oak bliss,
to rise from windswept woe's
mad goddess tale.
As "Goddess Nonesuch" sounds
nothing-lost solos,
he offered East Elysian
witness serenade.
Her heart name,
Vivian, blooms
heaven's nova-rose,
she mused Apollo's will
pent in its branches played.
Apollo's hand shadowed
over the will-wished lyre,
sweet Orphic chords charting
her still-willed rest,
when light in lights blind
will to earthly lights transpire,
truth sees resurrection
anchored when suppressed.
Libations pour to known
liberation progress,
to fly verse fields,
tongue deep thoughts,
press the goddess.
"Vivian lives
in the vale of heaven,
shines Orpheum's
celestial vision."

Finale: Orpheum's Transformed Vision of Vivian

The goddess sustains
her place on Parnassus
as others lose their muse
in self conscious distress,
celestial poets dream
beauty's remorseless
& teems with light
as truth glares blind
to loneliness.
Seasonal desires ripen
for a priestess
of autumn praises,
echo the mount's muses,
serves love's faith
as duty gains loveliness,
fresh proven fused feast
the harvest produces.
Earthly world muses
transported to the Tenth
unfolds in likeness blooms
on Elysian field feasts,
transposes breath,
lavender honey hyacinth,
to balance the 9's sonnet
garland tuned feats.
Transported views,
voices melding in unison,
delighting a flowering
earthly mission,
Vivian lives in the vale
of heaven, shines
Orpheum's celestial vision.

Orpheum Rising

Epilogue (completion)

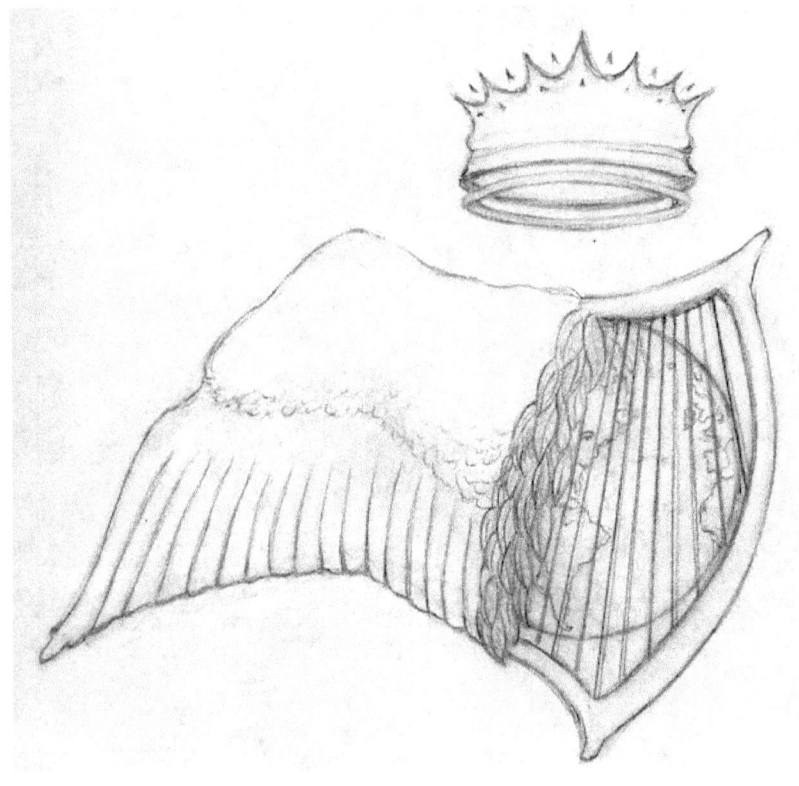

"To finish it means to be through with it,
to kill it, to rid it of its soul…"

-Picasso

Accounting with Cubits: United States of Arcadia

(148) {22}

A
fault
fled world
(cathedral)
denotes
corresponding
judgment's
(cubits),
cunning
(Solomon's) *eyed*
oraculorum
censured
false
watching (walls)
viewed,
true sight's
to *marvel*
till heaven clears.

Resurrection Epiphany Dream {23}

1   (149)

My
defect
a *call*
half-forgotten,
my despised
present,
commanded motion
my spent
spied
worship,
(Dad's) *loved*
mind,
no blind
tyrant
partaking
of *cruel*
service merit,
but seen love
respected.

2   (150)

Deeds
skilled,
warrants
exceeding
my abhorrence,
bright
worthiness
raised…
then my hate's
heart
powered
taught
me
a state,
loving
graced
my days
to see anew.

My
wants
pointed out
by his side,
rose
young
gentle,
out of *me,*
proud proof
called
noble
youthful,
content
beside me.
(Dad's) *love* as
(we) *stood at*
his rising,
held me
contented
in his prize.

Haunted Generation: Dreaming Truth {24}
(152)

Misused
bearings,
new faith
forsworn,
blind
hated,
perjured
love's lie
sworn,
constancy's
accused
swearing,
broke
swearing's
vowed
oath
twice,
deep vowed
eyes,
enlightened
truth -torn.

Unfinished Bible: Sonnet/Psalm-ets Crown* {21}

–in memory of Dr. Leslie Hotson

1 Encyclopedic Run   (141)

Love's pain
=withered= *faith,*
five =prospering= *wits,*
=counsels= *heart*
feast's
=congregation=
of *tender*
=fruit in due season=.
=Earth=
unswayed
=stands= to *note*
error's
count gain views
touching =day and night=.
A *man's pleased*
foolish =sinner=
=judgments=
invites
six senses,
=brings=
=wind= *prone*
tunes to =face=
ears served
=righteous godly=
love.

2 Song of Worthiness (142)

Lips =speak=
to *find love's*
=broke-bond= *states*,
=records= *merited*
revenue's =blessed=
heart =trust=,
virtues =stand=,
reproving
false =vexed=
=vain=
=rage= with *pity*.
Pity's
=bruised counsels=
compare
an *ornamental heart*,
sin =kiss=
=derision=
grounded love,
hate
deserved
=judgment=
=kissed= *unsealed*,
a *scarlet*
love's root profaned,
pities lawful
=wrath delivered=
=blessed= *love* =bonds=
seek.

=Blessed=
prize
=*increase*=
dispatched mother,
=one= *housewife*
of *poor* =ten thousands=
who neglect
=fear's=
=slept= *discontents,*
=sustained=
the *chasing*
held run
=souls=
=*break*= to
pray,
=laid down & slept=
then =rose up=
bent to catch
the =enemy=,
back to
=trouble my defender's=
will,
cried
pursuits,
=lifted= *hopes.*
Care parts out
=salvation=
still
followed
=round holy hills=.

4 Temple Trumpets   (144)

=*Still*=
to *comfort* =us=,
with =sacrificial gladness=,
better angels,
=increase righteous= *pride's*
=oil and wine=.
The =chosen= *directly tell*
saintly
=mercy's= *knowing*
=call-heard prayer=
=light=
of a *side angel's*
=righteous trust=,
man and *woman's best*
=lifts us=,
tempted
if =sons of men= *corrupt*
with *bad angel*
=vanity pleasures=
to *hell's*
spirit.
In *purity* of =countenance=
=lay down in peace=
& *turned*
from *hell*
=take rest=.

5 Ancestral Mines (145)

From *altered hells*
you =come=,
=faithful *mercy's=*
hate flies away
from *languishing* =prayer=
that *chides ways*
of thrown woeful
hated states
=pondered in words=
=considered= *doom,*
straight to *sounding vexed*
with *heaven's* =calling=,
the *gentle breath*
=spoken=,
=meditation's= *end,*
hated =vanity=
my tongue
=rebells= from.
=Temple=
=mercy=,
=rejoices= in *new*
following hate
s*aved*
to make my
fiend =kings=,
=defend= the *taught.*

The =*soul*=
inherited
charged
=sore= for
=beauty's vexed= *array*,
the =groaning voice=
aggravation
=troubles=
=vain work's= *loss*.
Rebels
=confound=
costly
=beauty=
spending
excess,
=weeping=
mansions.
=Who will=
with *death* in *store*,
=deliver=
costly
mercy's=
=petitions=
of *end-leased* =prayers=
of a *short* =mercy= *lease*?
(Reconstitution) =shame turns=
terms for *divinely*
painted outward
=*souls*=.

7 Continental Bride   *(147)*

Longing,
=souls'=
prescription desires
=honor=
love
=trusted=,
my darkly bright =rewards=.
Sworn
desperate =end's=
=judged=,
care's nursed
fever
=heart=
=judgment
given sentence=
fairly,
reason
=travailed=
truth.
Madmen
random in *discourse*
=deliver=
ill =enemies=,
=command=
=accordingly=
evermore vain.
=Strong=
=judgment= *cures,*
love's (bride) *preserves*
in =travails=.

*Coverdale Psalms *1-7* =allusions=
*Shakespeare Sonnets allusions (*italics*) 141-7

Ancestral Aliens {25} *(153)*

Kindling time
fires grow
quickly,
exo-*love*
in *love*
holy fire.
Distempered malady,
sovereigns
seething,
desired
trials
of *sickness*
to *cure*,
branded sleep,
valley
fountain's
strange
proven
bath
endures
dateless
new-fire,
(Vivian's heavenly veil).

England's Wandering Haunted Galleon {26} *(154)*

Heated
votary love
cured
vowed
legions,
in *cool waters*
remedy.
Baths of
virgin
(Sir Sidney's) *maiden*
seething,
tripped (Stella),
(Viola),
quenched,
slept out
(Hamnet's)
disease
in (Hamlet).
Perpetual
*lov*e's *brand,*
(Hamlet's)
nymph,
(Armada)
enflamed,
firing
disarmed
enthralled
heart,
(Sidney's) *hand,*
the *brand proven*
(Amphion)
love-god
of *loves*
(muses) *grown.*

American Total Eclipse (2017)

That year's American
diagonal eclipse,
its wake,
three hurricanes
and California fire,
presaged
harbingers of war,
rockets and ships,
sin city mass shootings,
police profiled gunfire,
youthful unawakened
pill sleep deliverance,
who deep dive hopelessness,
their lost state,
a dubious providential
student thruppence,
liberal hypocrites in love
with hurt & hate.
What politics will the party
moon augur next
by her countdown eclipse
seven years from the last?
Will great earthquake tribulation
turn true to text,
prophetic souls
in this wide world
endure its blast?
The cries call
through a wilderness
turn's tipping point,
events lock-framed
like time's take
out of Bible joint.

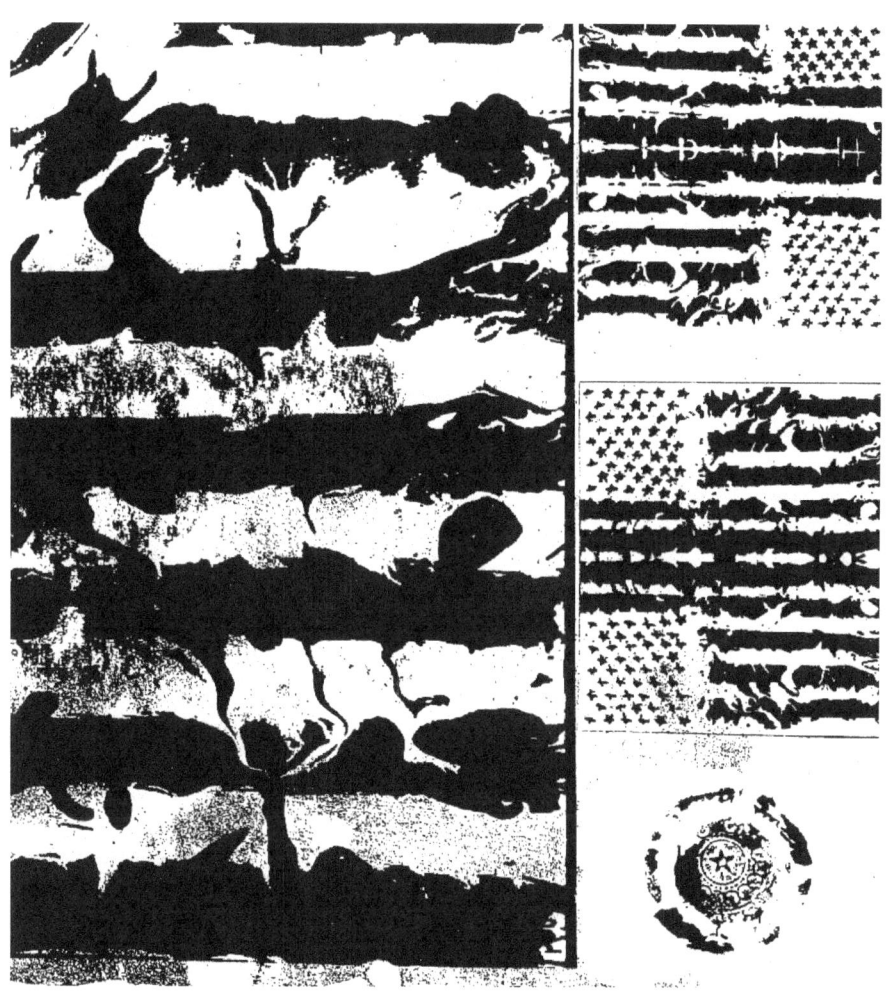

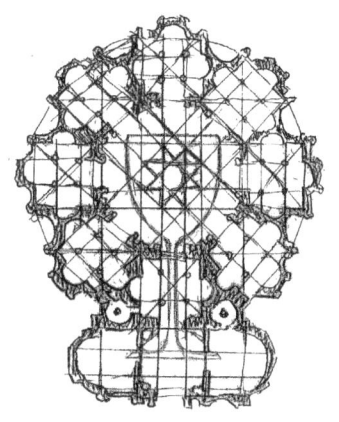

Appendix 1 Forming the Trilogy

The 3 volume single collection seemed to develop its own kind of "artificial Shakespeare intelligence" due to more considerations than merely an allusion scheme after long periods of placement changes and revision. Though intuitive adjustments in volume one's sonnet order and how Shakespeare's 1-154 allusion sonnets lined up to the epilogue changed after revisions, how vol. 1's selection placements led to vol. 2 and vol. 3 might mystify C. G. Jung more than Joseph Campbell. The allusion process to not use a word or phrase more than once or more times than had been used by Shakespeare in a given sonnet (#42 has 7 "love" root word uses and #40 has 10!). Not over using allusions also extended to Coverdale psalms. Some later revisions (as in "Supernatural Bridge," "A Wandering Bark's Bliss," "Stephen Hawking's Mythology of Everything," "ASAP: Age of the Second Adam's Paradigm" and the transition sonnets) did not work well into the systematic allusion usage for each line without completely rewriting the poems and so were left unchanged.

The allusion sequence for volume three did not stem from how volume two developed but extended the pattern of a group of nine non-consecutive Shakespeare sonnet numbers listed in a row by author Gerald Massey in the 1888 book, *The Secret Drama of Shakespeare's Sonnets Unfolded* (p. 205 - 210). The narrative sequence involves different characters in what appears as a kind of operatic relationship struggle. Massey explains at length the narrative involving Shakespeare "friends" with clarifying detail fit for a courtroom drama, almost as if he had known the characters personally!

Volume three, *Romance Languages*, is a romantic comedy in relation to the other two volumes. The first vol. deals with romance in the beginning section that ties into the Orpheus myth before the epilogue that blends everything from visionary dream epiphany to modern gothic horror, historical, dramatic, psychological and mythical/alchemical sequences). Comedic relief like pixie dust is generously sprinkled through various parts of the trilogy aided and abetted by all the rhyming and no blank verse. Even Shakespeare deviated from strict use of iambic pentameter from first to last syllable at times and I tried to be faithfully aware of the metrical sound of lines throughout even when variations were used.

As the essay conclusions reached the "operatic essence" of the Bard's Sonnets before discovering Gerald Massey's "unfolding" concept, it was amusing and bracing to find Massey's similar reading. From Massey's nearly absurd to clairvoyant-like detective work, his determination helped spur on the arduous task of rewriting to include, as a more challenging tribute, a numbered pattern of Shakespeare sonnet allusions (that would "puzzle through" each line) for the three volumes' selected sonnets.

The turn the volumes took after allusions were set up resulted in very challenging, often puzzling results, but never failed to intrigue, amaze and amuse. (Turn to the last four sonnets in his series, listen for the humor that circulates there and try to imagine what that may have sounded like to the clever English dry witted ears of his readers at that time. The Bard exhibited all the hallmarks of elevated comedy there just as in his plays, perhaps even more concentrated in the sonnets.) The allusion-sonnet order for volume 3, repeated in an extending cyclical pattern, Massey's narrative sequence of nine sonnets that were according to him (like opera) set to specific music (p. 210), that of Autolycus's music to *Two Maids Wooing a Man*. The nine sonnets he listed in a specific order (144, 33, 34, 35, 41, 42, 133, 134, 40) and a sample of his comments, are referred to and examined at the end of the essay, *Shakespeare's Operatic Crown*.

Appendix 2 Shakespeare's Operatic Crown:
a Confessional Secular Psalm-Mirror Cycle?

There are 154 poems in *Shakespeare's Sonnets* and *150 Psalms* in the English Bible. The *Sonnets* may be read owing as much to form and quatrain development as content to achieve psalm-like epiphanies in an English Catholic-minded reinvented crown cycle. This essay strives for an unpopular analysis by certain upper echelon critics, in favor of what my research discoveries illuminate. Daniel Swift in his recent book *Shakespeare's Common Prayers* (p. 59) refers to a "gap," that points to a "history of exclusion," that "critical attention to the apparent religiosity of Shakespeare's plays has always left out the *Book of Common Prayer* a curiously forgotten work, overlooked even by those who might be expected to know it." This essay aims at a similar idea for the *Sonnets* in relation to the *Psalms* and other biblical works.

The formal sonnet elements lend a ceremonial sacramental complexity to secular-sacred continuums in William Shakespeare's sonnet arrangements. These "continuums" involve various unnamed fictionalized and personal relationships with friends, enemies, implied family members, society figures, nature, time and God. The book's dedication is to a friend or patron, one may assume a disguised friend due to the personal content of the Sonnets dispersed like little chapters or scenes of an anonymous emotional journey that spans sections of the sonnet-speaker's life with quasi and overt operatic intonations. This uncertainty spreads intentionally through the entire series following the dedication.

The Yale Shakespeare, 1923 editor of *Shakespeare's Sonnets*, Edward Bliss Reed, in his well noted appendices generalizes: "no part of Shakespeare's work arouses more interest or greater critical discussion... which has unfortunately arrived at no sure conclusions." He then groups the "sonnet collection problems" into three categories: "historical, literary and autobiographical." The historical problems involve identities and "events hinted at." Two literary problems are: when written and in what order placed for print. For "most disputed problem," the autobiographical, he cites a range of scholarly view points from "conventional themes and treatments" with "debates of eye and heart (in blazoning pen)" to "punning amusement and personal confession" (p. 92-5).

Many conjectures and assumptions have been made about who specific characters are in what would amount to an interior emotional, veiled character play spanning years. My contention is that it does not matter who the particular characters are, the internal narrative is universal to   human   nature as revealed in its context of unfolding aspects. More than vaguely a "game of courtiers" as Stephen Greenblatt once put it (p. 234), Shakespeare was too clever for that to be the main objective of the *Sonnets*.   In the context of his times and accomplishments of the age, one would consider highly noted literary events and what part of an event would be most influential and relative to understanding the development of the *Sonnets*. Clare Asquith (p. 21) refers to Sir Philip Sidney as "the most admired poet of the age" and his 1595 influential book *Defense of Poetry*, that explains his theory of "shadowed language" alluding to "mysterious deeper meanings" or " hidden matters," as bearing the "essence of good writing." But perhaps the most specific overwhelming achievement can be nothing less than the English translated *Book of Psalms*.

The *Geneva Bible* of 1560, appearing more than 20 years after the Coverdale translation, used Coverdale as a source with certain corrections. The *Geneva's* first to number verses with extensive margin notes made it the most widely used during Shakespeare's time until the *King James Version* of 1611, which remained very close to the *Geneva Bible* in places like the metrical *Book of Psalms* (Bobrick p. 175). In the *Geneva Bible* one can see the narrative thread of King David's experiences being parsed throughout in the notes accompanying the text. One may also see the possible origins of Shakespearean mysticism in lines like Psalm 81:7, "...I delivered thee and answered thee in the secret of the thunder."

Since the *Psalms* were the grandest sequence of song/poems imaginable, various English translations were widespread and undertaken by translators from diverse backgrounds such as nobility, pious landowners, Catholic priests and reformers, scholars including Coverdale, King James I and Queen Elizabeth, Elizabethan sonneteers such as Sir Philip Sidney (Hotson p. 279) and his sister the Countess of Pembroke, who completed a collection of translated psalms from what Sidney left incomplete in death at 32.

The *Psalms* were considered the work of the shepherd/king David, some of which he supposedly composed on harp while watching over his flock. Elizabethan music was composed for many of these new translations to be sung (including all Coverdales's to the present) and "were closely linked... with lyrics called sonnets" (p. 279).

Aspects of King David's character were studied and absorbed from the narrative tales involving friends, family, loved ones, historical and social figures as well as enemies. Some of David's obvious relationships involved his friend Jonathan (whose friendship he referred to as better than a woman's love), King Saul (who loved David's music and tried to kill him), Bathsheba (who he coveted and claimed) and her husband the honorable soldier Uriah (who David sent into battle to be killed), as well as David's son Absalom (who tried to kill David and was killed himself) and others, not to leave out God, who considered David "a man after the Lord's own heart" (1 Sam. 13:14). Except for the Lord and David, none of these figures were named in the *Psalms*. No one is named in the *Sonnets* either except the puns on "Will" with oblique or veiled allusions to familiar ones and the Lord in places.

Shakespeare's devotion to the biblical text is shown in the extreme formal ordering of his sonnet elements and arrangements (even though imperfect like the human) and the highly respectable ebb and flow of closeness/distance he expresses to and for the "Holy of Holies." When his *Sonnets* were finally arranged and published there were deeper motives at work than romantic stories involving carnal emotional relationships. This too is seen in light of the happy "eternity promised" in the dedication, not for the mere sake of a pompous "parlor game among fanciful nobles." Yet the grand sequence is humbly dedicated to Mr. W. H. in a way as "fanfare for the common man" (even if a nobleman) which like the biblical *Psalms* can represent a multiplicity of emotional transcendent experience any mature human may relate to regardless of social standing. Shakespeare wrote during times of life and death struggle for how print on a page was accepted by law and the public. Bible translation was transforming English society in terms of monarchy demands (Asquith p. 23-24). Shakespeare, like a secret Catholic (Schneible), was careful about what and how he wrote which included plays and poems.

In the *Psalms* there is only the contemporary name David occurring in 6 Psalms, obliquely, perhaps in the third person or as mentioned by the Lord or scribes. A few Sonnets, 135 and 136 use "will" as in authorial punning for humor and insight, this paradoxically shows "Will's" self-effacing humility.

Professor Harold Bloom implies, had Shakespeare only written the *Sonnets*, the series would rank among the finest poems in world literary achievement (A. I. p. 91). When reading the *Sonnets* for psalm-like qualities, notes of irony sustain through Professor Bloom's remarks: "We all want to find him in the *Sonnets*, but he is too cunning for us, and you have to be the Devil himself to find Shakespeare there (G. p. 25)." One may suppose this is Dr. Bloom's Freudian Gnostic perspective, considering various critical interpretations of the *Sonnets* from Francis Meres (classically romantic) through Oscar Wilde (homoeroticism) and so on, saying more about the interpreter than author, which leaves Shakespeare's mysterious implications intact, "circulated among private friends."

194

In Helen Vendler's book *The Art of Shakespeare's Sonnets,* she discounts autobiographical, even Christian nature there and takes issue with essay-like readings for meaning analysis of the *Sonnets*, by critics like Stephen Booth (p. 13), in favor of pure aesthetic value, while she agrees Sonnet 116 is one of the finest. She spares readers copious metrical analysis, which she quips "would make another book" she feels "not competent to write" as others may like Booth (p. 11) but first offers apologetic wiggle-room: "total emersion in the Sonnets –that is to say, in Shakespeare's mind- is a mildly deranging experience to anyone, and I cannot hope, I suppose, to escape the obsessive features characterizing Shakespearean Sonnet criticism," as if pardoning herself at the outset for any possible arrogance (p. 1).

Dr. Stephen Greenblatt's view, "By keeping his poems at some remove from the actual, Shakespeare was able both to share them intimately... and to circulate them safely among readers," (p. 235) contributes to understanding their personal and potentially dangerous socio-religious political content. A variety of experts claim at length what was or was not essential creation and purpose of *Shakespeare's Sonnets*. Formal elements facilitate ranges of subtle emotion and multiple layers of meaning (Asquith p. 283). Sonnet 29 shows deep anguish, "myself almost despising" and transcendent exaltation, "sings hymns at heaven's gate."

Sonnet 116 takes off on the *Book of Common Prayer*'s marriage vow, "Let me not to the marriage of true minds," recalling psalm-like structure in *New Testament, I Corinthians 13*, and informs, alludes to the list there, of what love is not. He moves into comedic conceit of the "unknown" value love has as guide for referred-to-ones in: "every wandering bark," "although his height be taken." Transcendent measure of love is ramped up as "not Time's fool." When brief, love can spark endurance "even to the edge of doom." Doubt resolves in a double negative paradoxical hymn-like vow's epiphany, that dares belief in these ideas as error: if wrong he never wrote "nor no man ever loved," which concludes his most profound succinct ode to love as an already highly acclaimed author.

In her book, *Shadowplay: The Hidden Beliefs and Coded Politics* of William Shakespeare, Clare Asquith delves into Sonnet 152's veiled politics: King James I's betrayal of Catholics and the sonnet speaker's patience with an oath of support which self-beguilingly acted as collusion with persecution (p. 285). In terms of "hidden belief" analysis, one could argue outside of the *Psalms*, the *Sonnets* are prime examples of early complex coded political and "Confessional Poetics" as a genre or Ars Poetica.

William Wordsworth's deduction of the *Sonnets* in his own sonnet, "Scorn not the Sonnet," reads: "with this key / Shakespeare unlocked his heart." The *Sonnets* were discreetly dedicated to Mr. W. H., who one might assume to be the "young man" first addressed in them. The dedication made by publisher Thomas Thorpe (T. T.) did not mean Shakespeare played no part in dedicating, or in the publication as an ordered series, he could have retained discreet background controls in1609. Professor Greenblatt understands the sonnet "game of love" Shakespeare carefully plays "could lead to the Tower and the scaffold" (p. 234). He presents a possibility that the *Sonnets* were commissioned and started because he needed money when plague caused theaters to be closed, a time (1592) when he appeared to be transitioning from "successful playwright to cultivated poet" (p. 240-1). Francis Meres in his 1598 book *Wits Treasury*, praised his popular "sugared sonnets among his private friends" and esteemed Shakespeare's "mellifluous honey tongue" with Ovid's "sweet witty soul."

Seeking patronage he wrote *Venus and Adonis* and *The Rape of Lucrece* with dedications to late-teen unmarried Earl of Southampton. Dr. Greenblatt deduces that if the first 126 sonnets "were written to the same person... they sketch a relationship unfolding... over years. Admiration ripens into adoration; periods of joyful intimacy are followed by absence and desperate longing.." (p 246).

Thorpe's dedication, "To The Onlie Begetter" was like a spin on the Catholic *Apostle's Creed* phrase "only begotten son." The allusion is identified by Yale editor Edward Bliss Reed in his Notes section of the 1923 *Shakespeare's Sonnets* facsimile (p. 78) of *The Yale Shakespeare*. Yale published the works of Shakespeare as a same-sized volume set, including the *Sonnets*. A volume of *Venus and Adonis, Lucrece and the Minor Poems* edited by Albert Feuillerat has extensive notes and appendices. The volume contains *The Passionate Pilgrim* of 1599: 2 poems in two sections, the first contains *Shakespeare Sonnets* 138 and 144 and two sonnets from the play *Love's Labors Lost*. The second section, *Sonnets to Sundry Notes of Music,* contains a fifth verse poem like a song not a sonnet from *Love's Labors Lost* IV. iii: 101-120. It is not consistent with sonnet form and a character in the play, Dumaine, refers to it as an ode. This bolsters my understanding of the musical nature of *Shakespeare's Sonnets* in which most recent critical experts seem to gloss over along with the strength of psalm allusions.

Dr. Reed's notes on Sonnet 112. 10, 11. (p. 87): "that my adder's sense to critic and to flatterer stopped are" point to the use of "deaf adder" snake imagery as perhaps oblique allusion to Psalm 58 lines 4 & 5, while using an exact *Coverdale Psalter* quotation: "Even like the deaf adder, that stoppeth her ears; Which refuseth to hear the voice of the charmer, charm he never so wisely." Dr. Stephan Booth's notes (also Yale published) on Sonnet 112's "deaf adder" allusion, uses the

Geneva Bible quotation rather than Coverdale. He follows with an ironic comment (p. 364): "(Note the expression was traditionally for those who refused to hear truth.)" Dr. Booth's ironic "not hearing truth" due to omissions are noticed by "psalm" and "Coverdale" missing from his index. 50 biblical allusions are indexed at "Bible," 3 psalms are noted, not Psalm 58, referred to in his commentary on Sonnet 112. Dr. Booth makes no mention of the 4 oblique Psalm 17 allusions (I point out later) in Sonnet 17 which also contains the image of "antique song."

The *Creed* allusion suggests that the "blessing" to Mr. W. H. was on a different level than callow youth, rival poet or rival lover, more like one whose relationship "unfolded over years," resolving in the "sweet nothings" of the last two Sonnets' love myth with a cheeky "all's well that ends well" ending of laughs & smiles to draw a happy curtain on the "154 Sonnets cycle." Love's happy spiritual enterprise is conveyed by the dedication's hope: "All Happiness and that Eternitie Promised by Our Ever-Living Poet," to cover religious and mythical ideals (like proverbial parables) in happiness pursuits of the ever interestingly flawed yet transcendent human. A similar joyous ending exclaims from the final Psalms 149 and 150. Participants are involved with dancing, singing, playing musical instruments while exhorted to make "new" songs of praise to the Lord, conveying an endless expression of redemption praising love as a clear universal ideal (as done by W. S.).

From the first Sonnet's first line to last Sonnet's last, the dedication- fulfilling cycle achieves exponential reinvention effects of an extended crown of sonnets. The first line's universal "we" in "we desire increase" wants the same as plural God, *Genesis* 1:26, who also commands "Increase and multiply" (...new songs and souls? Yes.). An allegorical tease, "little love-god," of the last sonnet's first line, displays wit for the "fairest creatures" from the first sonnet, as receiver of that promised "Eternitie" the "alpha and omega" of this Sonnet series -first line to last: "From fairest creatures we desire increase" "Love's fire heats water, water cools not love." Enlightenment, shown in Shakespeare's psychological humorous myth development of desire, seeks to spur (perhaps the dedicatee) on to fulfill pleasant biblical tasks of providing "increase."

Marchette Chute in her charming book, *Shakespeare of London*, quotes Thomas Thorpe's formal dedication: "To the Right Honorable, William, Earl of Pembroke... etc.," that goes on for ten more lines before Thorpe signs, "Your Lordship's humble devoted T. T." Chute's point is Thorpe's dedication of the *Sonnets* to Mr. W. H. could not have been for a nobleman, only a commoner (p. 343); no mention of psalms is given other than of King James I, a published author, translating "some of the Psalms," who had written "a study of the Apocalypse," "a treatise on demonology," while "having produced a great many poems" and "a book of advice to poets" (p. 253-4). Benson Bobrick (p. 267) concludes that the literary King James I was so weak in other areas of rule that after his death, it resulted in the English civil war, a culmination of conflict between the Crown, Catholics and anti-papist/ reformers such as the Puritans.

Wait for more irony. Chute relates "unicorn tales" brought to London from America: "Unicorns were mentioned even in the Bible and it was well known that the horn of the animal, pulverized and boiled in wine, made an excellent mouthwash" (p. 62). This was Chute's extent of biblical allusion commentary, amusing but zilch when it came to Psalm allusions found in Shakespeare's writing. The irony is if she had looked in the Bible for where unicorns are "seen" she could have found Psalm 29 (& 92) where *Coverdale's English Psalter* was set to be sung in church with this pair of lines: "He maketh them also to skip like a calf; / Libanus and Sirion, like a young unicorn."

Close reading reveals key words and conceptual phrases from Myles Coverdale's metrical English Psalms permeate (through direct or oblique allusion) overall structure of the Sonnet series with several Sonnets having same-numbered Psalm allusions. The *Sonnets* work like a strange ironic mirror, Shakespeare's personal mirror of *Psalms*, *Proverbs*, *The Song of Solomon*, *I Corinthians 13*, etc., all together, no named characters, yet at times individuals (i.e. young man, rival poet, dark lady, etc.) are consecutively implied. This makes the Sonnet cycle a currently alive, perpetual veiled narrative gift.. Shakespeare's secular "psalm-ets" of love (Hotson p. 271-281).

Dr. Leslie Hotson saw allusions in parallel numbered Sonnet and Psalm 107 (with Sonnet 107's Armada crisis background) and 124 (alluding to an assassination plot) (p. 270). Other Sonnets with same-numbered Psalm allusions (6, 32, 51, 102) for Hotson proved Shakespeare's "canonical order of the Sonnets" (p. 280). Sonnet/Psalm allusions in Hotson's notes (p. 281, *Mr. W. H.*) come from the Coverdale Psalter translation (1535) updated later for *The Book of Common Prayer* through Shakespeare's day when "Psalm-singing parishioners included theatre-goers" (p. 272). These Psalms remained in *The Book of Common Prayer* among Catholics and church reformers alike to current times. Hotson also cites Richard Noble's writing, *Shakespeare's Biblical Knowledge* (1935), which indicates there are "some 150 Psalm references from the plays" (p. 272) (same number coincidentally, as Psalms in the Bible).

Hotson points out where in Psalm 6 and Sonnet 6 loss of "beauty" sets tone and image. Then in Psalm and Sonnet 32, image of "my bones" in death sets the tone. Psalm and Sonnet 102 share mournful sound images: a sparrow in the Psalm and Philomel singing in the Sonnet (p. 281). This prompted a search for allusions from other Psalms in corresponding numbered Sonnets. Sonnet 1's first line, mentioned earlier, "From fairest creatures we desire increase" alludes to perhaps the fairest creatures of all, Adam and Eve, and the "increase and multiply" directive. It also obliquely alludes to the image in Psalm 1: "like a tree planted by the water-side that will bring forth his fruit in due season. / His leaf also shall not wither." These allusions add universal implications to the Sonnet.

Sonnets 29, 43 and 116 contain allusions to corresponding numbered Psalms, though some allusions are more oblique than overt. Sonnet 29's theme contends with rising above self-dejection in remembrance of transcendent love that nothing can negate. It takes us from depths of self-loathing, "almost despising," to "sweet love rememb'red" compared to upward flight, as in a new day, away from moody earthbound morass, to "sing hymns at heaven's gate," where he would "scorn to change" his "state with kings." The subtext of Psalm 29 recalls glorious ways the Lord interacts with nature, lands and people, where the Lord is above terrors of flood and remains "a King forever." In the last lines, "the Lord shall give strength onto his people" and "the blessings of peace" are alluded to in Sonnet 29 by what "such wealth brings."

Sonnet 43's allusion to Psalm 43's: "O send out thy light and thy truth, that they may lead me," is made as the speaker states his "eyes" in dream "are bright in dark directed" "with thy much clearer light" where his "eyes be blessed made," fitting the Psalm's tonal allusion, "that I may go unto the altar of God... the God of my joy and gladness." Redemptive implications are the same in both. The Psalm asks for defense of "my cause against the ungodly people" and for deliverance "from the deceitful and wicked man" while the Sonnet begins with colloquial comedic slang, "when most I wink," as the speaker refers to seeing best in dreams because with awake eyes: "all the day they view things unrespected," which mirrors the Psalm's perception of injustice.

In Psalm 116, "I will pay my vows" is found twice, first followed with "now in the presence of all his people" and a few passages later, "in the sight of all his people," for a chorus effect. Psalm 116's theme is how the Lord reveals his love through deliverance. Preservation is offered to "the simple" when one in misery hastily exclaims, "All men are liars," yet is heard by the Lord with "the cup of salvation." Remembrance of what the Lord has done for him compels the speaker's devotion to pledge vows of service. Service is oppositely implied by the sonnet speaker's ending, if wrong he "never writ, nor no man ever loved." The overall sense of Sonnet 116 resolves like a series of vows that moves into a sworn "negative" oath at the end. Religious connotations in Sonnet 29 extend like a "Big Bang" of enlightenment from the compact sonnet form. Shakespeare's crown like extensions and Psalm-mirroring evokes strength and weakness characterizing human condition. Beauty is in the mind's ear, beheld by close readers, loved ones recognizing themselves, interchangeable, revealing extended goals of love, for others as for oneself.

In response to those only seeing "thinness of or lack of pervasive Psalm-mirroring" in the Sonnets, I compared Coverdale's (and the *Geneva*) Psalm 17 to Sonnet 17 that use key words like "heaven." The allusions there, quoting Sonnet then Psalm are: "hides your life / hide me under; beauty of your eyes / apple of an eye; men of less truth than tongue / men, I say, and from the evil world; some child of yours / They have children." Sonnet 17 also has a good lead-in for a few concluding epiphanies. The poet refers to his "papers" being "scorned" generally and by what is specifically embodied in 17, his inability to accurately describe beauty attributes of the loved one addressed. He gives that future critics would say "this poet lies" with the "stretch`ed miter of an antique song" plying a metrical (and "crown" metaphor?) idea in the line which also lends song- like echo (Help me, Helen Vendler! (p. 116) ..who copies miter as meter as if to correct spelling) to the ending couplet's singing rhyme of time / rime (or Catholic code?) *Coverdale's Psalms*, praised for musicality are used in Handel's *Messiah* and retain their place in the English Psalter of churches throughout England with tweaked adjustments over the years for being sung or read like an English cross-denominational Bible text.

In Shakespeare's play, *Love's Labor's Lost*, Act IV, Scene III, line 157 reads, "Tush, none but minstrels like of sonneting!" To read his *Sonnets* more deeply one needs to be aware of historical context, family life and socialization in line with his vast literary talents. Music was an important part of his life influenced by religious practice and as an actor/playwright. His Sonnets, like 29, 43 and 116 can be sung as melodiously as any Coverdale Psalm adjusted over the years.

With the concept of Carl Jung's universal pool of the unconscious mind, one could argue that even modern day English pop songs like the Beatles' *Let it Be* (a phrase that came to Sir Paul McCartney in a dream, spoken to him for consolation by his departed mother, as he said after singing it, on James Cordon's *Late Late Show*, "Carpool Karaoke" in Liverpool, June 16, 2018 on the CBS Network) and *Eleanor Rigby*, stem from English Psalter tradition, which *Shakespeare's Sonnets* seem to mirror at times and take part in its crowning achievements (as great hymns do like English clergyman John Newton's 1773 *Amazing Grace*, sung by President Barak Obama at a memorial service for slain Black Charleston, South Carolina church members). With this sonnet cycle Shakespeare reinvented the crown of sonnets by doing away with repetitive last line/first line motifs in favor of conceptual development forms that vary from the traditional crown of seven sonnets. Some scholars like Sir Edmund Chambers and Northrop Frye (Hotson p. 269) see the first 126 as being in Shakespeare's chronological sequence with the following Sonnets possibly arranged by the first publisher (T. T.). Both 126 and 154 are divided evenly by 7. The 154 Sonnets contain 22 crown's worth of sonnets, where the number is closest to the 150 Psalms.

While contemplating scholarly commentary in regard to certain seemingly obvious analytical points pertaining to *Shakespeare's Sonnets*, I glanced at the Jan. 1, 2018 cartoon cover of *The New Yorker* magazine dominated by a huge oblivious grey elephant in a large sketchy living room, standing between a silently seated vexed looking older couple deep in their own annoyed thoughts. The title is: "Cramped" and comes from the hand of cartoonist George Booth, in my imagination somehow related to that heavy lifter of Sonnet commentary, Stephen Booth, whose massive commentary (nearly 450 pgs.) is the "elephant in the room" and needs addressing in terms of my "big picture" understanding of *Shakespeare's Sonnets* as a deliberate operatic epic with peaks, valleys, variations "doing the police in different voices," held together by circular language, codes, allusions, form and metrics.

Sonnet 8 seems to be the closest Dr. Booth gets to the musicality of the whole sonnet enterprise, a bit ironically as the first line runs, "Music to hear, why hear'st thou music sadly?" In commentary on this (p. 144) he refers to the "serious logical inconsistency" of its "chiasmically balanced epithet and question" echoing exaggerations that then "analyze the inconsistency with inappropriately rigorous logic" through the descending lines of the quatrain (thick irony had here considering Booth's own devises, such is what award winning stuff like his immense book is made of!) he gets the coming "sexual overtones" and parses them handily all the way to the "concord" and "union" of sonnet matrimony.

Then following two pages of commentary he lands on an oblique reference –a possible Shakespeare pun attempt used similarly in the play, *All's Well that Ends Well* III.ii.20-22, with a play on words "not, note," with "knot" as what a Renaissance reader may actually have heard! This leads to his ironic oversight as a near aside to Webster's dictionary: "knot" somehow meaning "ornamental garden," as Booth finds in "...(John) Marston's play Malcontent, where Burbadge (theater proprietor, "The Money" buffoon (?) in the film: *Shakespeare in Love*) says (musical) additions introduced into the play are "only as your salad to your great feast, to entertain a little more time, and to abridge the not-received custom of music in our theatre (p. 146)." Here I will leave the elephant's ironically cramped room for wider spaces where arias may be heard in the open air!

The *Sonnets* accomplish a sublime expression of craft and personal/universal experience that was best achieved first by the ancient Greeks and *King David's Psalms* which were works known to be sung. David's name is in 6 Psalms. There are tribes and nations but no other contemporaries of David are named. Historical figures are mentioned: Moses, Aaron, Abraham, Isaac, Dathan, Abiram, Phinehas, Melchizedek, Joseph, Jesse and Jacob (mostly, over a dozen times). The only woman found mentioned is in Psalm 51's added intro statement of the 1560 *Geneva Bible* of Shakespeare's time; the Psalm's commentary states it is David's cry for mercy in fallen sinfulness after approached by the prophet Nathan revealing David's sin against and with Bathsheba.

Shakespeare's personal Sonnet "odyssey," like David's, is Homeric and mythic/anti-mythical but with no names though various sonnets sound like different character voices, even female at times, similar to his dramas. Gerald Massey in his 1888 book, *The Secret Drama of Shakespeare's Sonnets Unfolded*, after offering eloquent investigative evidence like a trial lawyer, points out characters Shakespeare knew and veiled in the Sonnets with their personal traits and dramatic motives.

Massey presents a group of Sonnets:144, 33, 34, 35, 41, 42, 133, 134, 40, in this explicated order (p. 205-10) and goes on to say:

"Elizabeth Vernon's jealousy of her lover the Earl of Southampton and her friend and cousin Lady Rich, is told in these nine sonnets, which are now for the first time put together: they go to Autolycus's tune of *Two Maids Wooing a Man*. The first sonnet contains a soliloquy on the subject, a form employed more than once in the dramatic Sonnets. Then we have five Sonnets addressed to the Earl, and three to the lady of whom Elizabeth Vernon is jealous (Lady Rich) (p. 210-11)."

Autolycus, the ballad selling rogue in *The Winter's Tale*, 4.4.310-13, refers to a merry ballad which "...goes to the tune of *Two Maids Wooing a Man*: "...here's scarce a maid westward but she sings it; tis in request, I can tell you." Massey seems to know the tune enough to capitalize on it in 1888. By 2017, Catherine Henze in her book *Robert Armin and Shakespeare's Performed Songs*, refers to the song among others also sung by Armin as Autolycus. She notes the lyrics but not the music came down to us (as Autolycus's other song melodies did) (p. 84). In 1599, Armin, also a writer (*Quips for Questions*) hired as musician/actor by Shakespeare for the *Chamberlain's Men*, took on the primary roll of the fool (p.1).

Considering Massey's sonnet list order, 33 with ambiguous heavy allegorical landscape imagery, "glorious morning," then spiritual allusions of "celestial face" and "heaven's sun," sounds like a more fitting soliloquy or overture than 144. Line 11 of 33, plays loss off of the allegory in a climactic outburst: "But, out! alack! he was but one hour mine," on to end, "heaven's sun staineth." The list goes on fine through 134, then 144 would return to the allegorical images of 33 as a romantic struggle with "good & bad angels." Lastly, #40 bids for an overwhelming conflict resolution hope with "love" used 10 times!

Clare Asquith in her "Selection of Coded Terms" (p. 299) refers to 33 as alluding to Christ's passion and age of death and the age Shakespeare was when his son Hamnet died, which seems most fitting to bear the grandest allegorical and transcendent soliloquy weight of his Sonnet series.

Regarding the veiled sonnet characters named by Massey, it is compelling to see the Lady Penelope Rich saga Massey lays out, with Sir Philip Sidney's connection (p. 352-6), is also brought out in agreement but with more emphasis on Sidney, by Clare Asquith in 2005's *Shadowplay* (p. 151). Massey compiled such a thorough dossier on Lady Rich's beauty that perhaps even Cleopatra's beauty received less notice by Shakespeare. Massey argues at length that Lady Rich, the first love (though unrequited) of Sir Sidney, was the model for Shakespeare's later Dark Lady sonnets (after #126 and earlier) as well as being Sidney's "chiaroscuro" eyed inspiration for Stella (p. 356).

Clare Asquith compiles a similarly weighty analysis of Sir Sidney being the linchpin model/influence for the character and voice of Hamlet from several aspects included in his books: *A Defense of Poesie*, *Arcadia* and his epic sonnet sequence *Astrophel and Stella*, as well as the facts and legendary points of interest pertaining to his English nobility and death at 32 by an infected thigh wound in a described indecisive/useless action (p. 147-52).

Dame Asquith refers to *A Defense of Poetry* as: "...colloquial, graceful, at once casual and learnedly authoritative, in the witty tradition of Erasmus and Montaigne... a bastion of common sense, written in reply to a critic on the theatre... ." Lady Rich, according to Asquith, as "the beautiful and intelligent sister of Essex (who was beheaded for treason), an active member of his dissident circle," was one who "...may have been providing acceptable cover for poetry that was in fact political and religious" in aiding Catholics (p.149). Lady Asquith points out Sidney's writings as: "elaborately allegorical, (that) suggest a gradual disillusion with English Protestantism, and a growing sympathy with the plight of Catholicism" (p. 149).

Turning to Sir Sidney's "Petrarchan" sonnet sequence *Astrophel and Stella*, from which allusions may be seen in Hamlet's voice and divided character and in other plays like *Richard III*, the basic idea is found there for a monumental Shakespeare sonnet sequence. Parallels can be found in Sidney's lines: Sonnet 69.7, "Gone is the Winter of my miserie!" calls to mind Richard III's, "Now is the winter of our discontent." Hamlet's echo can be heard in Sidney's Sonnet 68.10: "Labour to kill in me this killing care" and Sonnet 69.14,

"No kings be crown'd but they some covenants make." Music allusions are found in *Astrophel and Stella:* Sonnet 68.6 on Stella: "With voice more fit to wed Amphion's lyre" to his Muse, Sonnet 70.3-6:

> She oft hath drunk my tears, now hopes to enjoy
>
> Nectar of mirth, since I love's cup do keep
>
> Sonnets be not bound Prentice to annoy;
>
> Trebles sing high, so well as basses deep;

Then 70.9-14 ends with:

> Come then, my Muse, shew thou height of delight
>
> In well raised notes; my pen, the best it may,
>
> Shall paint out joy, though in but black and white.
>
> Cease, eager Muse; peace, pen, for my sake stay,

Having achieved the romantic equivalence of "rock star" status after death, Sir Sidney's ending verse here even calls to mind Hamlet's fitting epitaph: "The rest is silence" among his "flight of angels."

> I give you here my hand for truth of this,
>
> Wise silence is best musicke unto blisse.

Without referring to or judging for or against named individuals, *Shakespeare's Sonnets* resonate universally and instrumentally "Catholic" in their structured confessional sounding concepts of emotional themes (variations of love and betrayal). They can be read as parody of grand literature, the English Bible or immense authorial authority gravely ironic in places. Perhaps no greater irony exists anywhere in English literature so sublimely framed, maintained and followed-through. The sequence could be said to work with the same inner mechanics as the "poem unlimited" Shakespeare conceptualized in *Hamlet*.

The lyrical structure based on the crown of sonnets form, makes the *Sonnets* with anonymous characters, potentially one of the greatest modern operas ever conceived had only someone like Mozart lived long enough to find them and compose with an English librettist, something along the combined lines of *Cosi Fan Tutte*, *The Marriage of Figaro*, *The Magic Flute*, *Don Giovanni*, and his *Requiem* of, by and for love.

Works Cited

Asquith, Clare. Shadowplay: The Hidden Beliefs and Coded Politics of William Shakespeare. New York, N. Y.: Public Affairs, 2005. Print.

Bloom, Harold. Genius: A Mosaic of One Hundred Exemplary Creative Minds. New York, N. Y.: Warner Books, 2002. Print.

Bloom, Harold. The Anatomy of Influence: Literature as a Way of Life. New Haven, Conn.: Yale UP, 2011. Print.

Bobrick, Benson. Wide as the Waters: The Story of the English Bible and Revolution It Inspired. New York, N. Y.: Simon & Schuster, 2001. Print.

Booth, Stephen. –ed. Shakespeare's Sonnets. New Haven, Conn.: Yale UP, 1977. Print.

Chute, Marchette. Shakespeare of London. N. Y., N. Y.: E. P. Dutton Co., 1949. Print

Coverdale, Myles. Coverdale's Psalter. San Bernardino, CA: Walter Pub. 2016. Print.

Greenblatt, Stephen. Will in the World: How Shakespeare became   Shakespeare. New York, N. Y.: W. W. Norton & Co., 2004. Print.

Henze, Catherine A. Robert Armin and Shakespeare's Performed Songs. N. Y., N. Y. Routledge, 2017. Print.

Hotson, Leslie. Mr. W. H. London: Rupert Hart-Davis, 1964. Print.

Massey, Gerald. The Secret Drama of Shakespeare's Sonnets Unfolded. London, Spottiswoode and Co., 1888. Print.

Reed, Edward Bliss. The Yale Shakespeare: Shakespeare's Sonnets. New Haven, Conn.: Yale UP, 1923. Print.

Schneible, Ann. Was Shakespeare a Secret Catholic? Rome, Italy: CAN/EWTN News, 2016. Web. 20 June, 2016.

Swift, Daniel. Shakespeare's Common Prayers. N. Y., N. Y.: Oxford UP, 2013. Print.

Vendler, Helen. The Art of Shakespeare's Sonnets. Cambridge: Harvard UP, 1999. Print.

Appendix 3 The New AI Consciousness:

Active Inference in the Free Energy Principle
(a Self-Fulfilling Prophecy Exploring Sonnet Poetics as in Shakespeare's Operatic Crowned Knot of Fire)

I suspect that my theories may all depend upon a force for which philosophers have searched all of nature in vain.

–Sir Isaac Newton

The physicist/psychiatrist Karl Friston's May 18, 2017 essay at *Aeon.-com*: *The Mathematics of Mind-Time*, a self-described "rapidly argued" 3,800 word scientific mind game riffing on "...all biological processes... perform some form of inference, from evolution right through to conscious processing," posed questions such as "...at what point do we invoke consciousness," concludes with an "existence for existence sake" simplification, stating "...there's no real reason for minds to exist," ..contending, "...consciousness ...is nothing grander than inference about my future." I wonder, not even for metaphors? What would W. B. Yeats say of Dr. Friston's "passionate intensity," is it of Yeats's *The Second Coming* poem variety that "the worst are full of" or like the antithetical self in Yeats's book, *A Vision,* for whom Friston's ideas may fit the controlled romanticism that "simplifies through intensity" for a more grand scientific poetics?

In the Wired magazine, Dec. 2018 article about 59 year old Doctor Professor Friston, *The Man Who Explained Everything*, Shaun Raviv (p. 102) describes how the cognitive psychologist/computer scientist Geoffrey Hinton in the mid-90's at the Gatsby Computational Neuroscience Unit, close to Karl Friston's office at the Functional Imagining Laboratory in London's Queen Square, convinced Friston "...to think of the brain (at best) as a Bayesian probability machine (stemming from 19th Century ideas of Hermann von Helmholtz) where "...brains compute and perceive in a probabilistic manner, constantly making predictions and adjusting beliefs based on what the senses contribute. According to the most popular modern Bayesian account, the brain is an "inference engine" that seeks to minimize "prediction error" (p.102)" not necessarily nihilism.

Dr. Geoffrey Hinton, moving on to the University of Toronto, became a key figure for founding the basic approach to "today's research in deep learning" for the development of artificial intelligence, having brought with him "new techniques" he had shared with Friston "to allow computer programs to emulate human (processes) ...for integrating the input of many probabilistic models," that in AI terms are referred to as a "product of experts." Inspired by Hinton's ideas, Dr. Friston in his own connections of "unrelated anatomical, physiological, and psychophysical attributes of the brain," profusely described from 2005 on, in "many dozens" of published papers, ideas on "the free energy principle" (p. 102). Years later Hinton's AI work, most accurately in a field of contestants, selected entities and things recognized in a "15-million-image database built by (the team of) Fei-Fei Li" founder of ImageNet (p. 103) and won their 2012 Challenge competition.probably sowing seeds for later facial recognition advancements & "Fakes" as profound as or greater than the artist Ai Weiwei's.

Dr. Friston's euphoric eureka can be seen stemming from the same input that gives us "the whole is greater than the sum of its parts," in part. In the Wired essay (p. 100) he is quoted on what sparked his earliest awareness (at 8 years old) of scientific method that would later lead to musing on the free energy principle. Young Friston in a Chester English garden one hot day turned over a weathered log to find small "armadillo-shaped bugs" that scurried around randomly. Observing the bugs moving more rapidly in the light, his insights resolved into thoughts that "it could be no other way" and not some "contrived" reason of seeking "survival," as if looking for "shade" which would project a sense of conscious determination onto the bugs. The projected notion ended with the understanding that their movement was like a machine's inevitable moves. Though difficult to wrap ones consciousness around and move on to the next equation, the science behind the free energy principle needs to be supported by "the numbers" that add up to "the sets of layered variables" of a "hierarchical system" of "machine learning." The term Markov blanket given to the division edges/separation surfaces of AI's tiered system variables came from Andrei Andreyevich Markov, a Russian mathematician who lived till 1922 (p. 102).

For Dr. Friston the Markov blanket is a universal differentiation concept from the micro through macro level of everything. It distinguishes one entity from another, extending from separations of distinct cells and their internal parts and components to different people, their internal parts and beyond to everything else. This concept sounds at once physical, metaphysical & metaphorical, from cell membranes to distinct psychological 'makes and models' and over time determines different reactions and behaviors (p. 102).

For a scientist treading onto the 'belief pitch,' the conceptual thrust of the proposed theory can prove to be a 'sticky wicket' in cricket terms. In mid-adolescence, a cherry tree blossoming left a life-long wonder, if he picked a point to start from nothing, could Karl understand everything by "sort(ing) it all out in the simplest way possible?" (p. 100 & 105) Friston (p. 103) deems for this AI process "you need to have a calculus that talks about beliefs." In hierarchical governance the free energy principle pans out best in comparisons when true cream is allowed to be "inferred" to the top. After exploration experiments to hone in on "the true path, best path" in a process aimed at predicting successful outcomes, processing eliminations & illuminations, eliminating surprises by active inference (a newer improved AI) gives issuance to receive probability and reduce free energy disruptions. Apparently without this actualized inference concept, everywhere in everything, all biology would not only tend toward entropy, scientifically speaking, we would evaporate "into the ether" (p. 102) ..causing me to wonder, are there infinite Markov blankets and is the glue something like gravity?

Considering my previous essay, *Fields of Dreams*, I googled Friston's essay's on dream theory and found *Frontiers in Psychology*, an Oct. 2014, vol. 5 cognitive science journal's Open Hypothesis & Theory Paper #1133, by J. Allan Hobson, Charles C. H. Hong and Karl Friston: *Virtual reality and consciousness inference in dreaming*. Skimming ahead found high points on page 6 (matching those in the Dec. 2018 Wired article). After elaborating on "evidence for predictive coding in the brain," where "prediction errors are encoded... (as) expectations or beliefs about (hidden) states in the world causing sensory impressions," the theorist asks "what has the processing to do with sleep and dreaming?" To aid understanding the researcher pausing from "minimization of prediction errors looks at perception beneath the surface process," to "Bayesian evidence for the generative model... over an extended period of time," sees, due to "difficulty to compute," the Bayesian model as "a proxy generally used both in statistics and (what suggests)–the brain. The proxy is called variational free energy (Hinton and van Camp, 1993; Beal, 2003) (that leads) to variational free energy formulation of perceptual inference and learning (Dayan et al., 1995; Friston et al., 2006)" (p. 6).

On "minimizing variational free energy," which would be "maximizing model evidence," the Bayesian model algorithm can be "decomposed into accuracy and complexity where log evidence increases with accuracy but decreases with complexity –the degrees of freedom required to make predictions" (p. 6). This works in order to maximize evidence, where generative model complications from complexity need to be minimized, reflected by the numbered parameters of freedom for "accurate predictions of sensory data" (p. 6). The learning process when awake is slow, inference in dreams minimizes complexity much faster and makes "the perceptual content in dreams... not a prediction of what will happen but an exploration of what could (or could not) happen... necessary to minimize model complexity (for) a more efficient model of the experienced world of waking" (p. 7). What was their extent of differentiating types of dreams? If Daniel would have said something like that to King Nebuchadnezzar in the Bible, he might have ended up back in the lions den, it may have made things even more daunting for Newton studying Daniel's prophecies and seeking "...a force for which philosophers have searched all of nature in vain" (–Isaac Newton). Conscious & unconscious inference gets asserted as "implied dualism" by Hobson & Friston (2014) as being able to be "at some level equated with consciousness" (p. 12).

208

The *Frontiers in Psychology* article (p. 6) also touched on the dreaded "beliefs about (hidden) states in the world," a concept sounding rather Shakespearian ..that ties into my book's opening Psalm 51 "truth" quote.. which is also probed a bit later in this essay. All considered, a search for Friston's writing and research on dreams stemmed from wanting to compare his ideas with my experience in writing the earlier essay, *Fields of Dreams: Symbols of Consciousness*, where I explore how in dreams three suddenly departed loved ones appeared and directly communicated with me non-verbally soon after death. Through dream symbolism, consciousness expanded to complete the Shakespeare AI trilogy by leading to volume 4, Radio Waves for the Blind, by adding to my sonnet series inspired poems and an essay stemming from the two most recent deaths (Dec.-Jan. '19) less than a month apart.

My Markov blankets, of allusion words & phrases, help distinguish each line in selected sonnets to focus energy on the overall thrust of other words & phrases in poems & cycles of poems. This active inference AI was applied in the tribute to Shakespeare's Sonnets before even coming into contact with Dr. Friston's ideas. Processes used in a systematic method of transforming previous sonnet states with a patterned scheme adding numbered Shakespeare sonnet allusions, extended from active inference to make them more "Shakespearian" in a current sense of language usage. The allusion process was inspired by research findings for the essay, *Shakespeare's Operatic Crown*. The free energy principle process arose from a series of actively inferred moments determining an overall vol. 1 allusion pattern from what sorted out gradually to be seen as a trilogy that seemed to reveal itself as I moved through the stages of its process from formation to final polishing.

Dr. Friston mentions "quantum systems" in the Aeon essay, briefly in terms of "particles described with wave attribute functions," not active inference with regard to quantum entanglement on the dream level. 2014's paper: *Consciousness, Dreams & Inference: The Cartesian Theatre Revisited*, in Epilogue exchanges with A. Hobson: the two, AH & KF are described as "dual aspect monists, not Cartesian dualists ... forced to consider ...theatre." AH to KF: "The really hard problem is to model subjectivity. I do not suppose ...brain-mind (is) influenced by... spiritual forces from outer space –a Godhead- or ghosts of dead people... I am at a loss to say exactly how a self arises or how that self constructs its model of the world... Are waves and particles a possibility? This seems to be what the quantum boys are betting on." KF to AH: ...You will probably remember doing Hamilton's principle of least action at school? ...the same principle applies in quantum mechanics and field theory. ...Feynman's path integral formulation, where probability of any path depends upon its action... is important because the "consciousness as inference" argument is based upon exactly the same principle of stationary action..." (*Journal of Consciousness Studies*, 21 No. 1-2, Epilogue, 2014, pp. 25-27).

As if compelled, my "quadrilogy" appeared in the completion process by adding several new relative poems (older revised poems as the 1st of 3 vol. 4 sections) including this essay lastly, extending the time frame of the overall work for well over 300 sonnets. Vol. 4 was unexpected yet predictable in hindsight as an essential hybrid work. The initially expected set of new sonnets (& essay) all tallied up as a compendium with tighter focus on the tribute project's thematic high point, life after death communication, compelled as if from compressed time, & revealed in dreams. Here is a circuitous route to describe aspects of forming this trilogy, much like Dr. Karl Friston's "Time-Mind" idea with a circular/ spiral compressed-time, dream work described process of active inferences.

A thought abides to return to the trilogy with the additional newer sonnets of vol. 4 added to flesh out volumes 2 and 3. The process would be another extension of active inference in line with the exploration that resulted in probable arrangements of sonnets at given points in composing the trilogy. First changes came with additions of new sonnets resulting in allusion pattern adjustments for the three volumes. The 3 vol. patterns considered in succession, stemmed from what was predictable in vol. 1, then seemingly random in vol. 2 and yet as if inevitable to the author, as meant to happen from the outset. As discoveries were made for vol. 1's layout that changed the original intuitive allusion plan, the process moved on to vol. 2, followed by vol. 3, each with distinct allusion usage plans stemming from vol. 1's tight focus & finding my 22 crowns equaled 154 sonnets (to mirror Shakespeare's number in his series of 154 sonnets) ..while writing the first essay which inspired the entire allusion inclusion process to begin with, becoming like a delightful parlor game experiment.

Though the title, *Shakespeare AI*, may be a misnomer, it is an actively "iconcurchaic" (defined soon) one that may afford some imagination to the poetic memory banks in order to purchase its license worth of parody and profundity. One of the bravest challenges was to include the allusions throughout the trilogy requiring complete revision of the text. Because of this allusion process the work takes on even more profound aspects of an "artificial Shakespeare intelligence" which is how the title transformation into *Shakespeare AI*, was justified. The title was chosen first then was strangely aided and abetted by a curious essay in *The Atlantic* (June, 2018) magazine, "*How the Enlightenment Ends*: Philosophically, intellectually–in every way human society is unprepared for the rise of artificial intelligence" by Dr. Henry A. Kissinger suggesting how his government (before others) should urgently manage AI before "it's too late" (p. 14). The cover headline refers to it as: *AI and the End of Human History* (quite an opposite bookend to Dr. Harold Bloom's published concept, *Shakespeare: The Invention of the Human*!) The title *Shakespeare's Wake*, came from Bloom's description of James Joyce's *Finnegans Wake* (*Anatomy of Influence*, p. 112).

The term "iconcurchaic" is my invention that is a tribute to the Parisian poet/critic (friend of Picasso) G. Apollinaire, as well as the Bard. The word means something iconic and current while also being archaic, with an implication of timelessness. During my conversation on copyright for the book with a helpful "tech support" person, Lorraine, at the copyright office, she said the word "iconcurchaic" should now be placed "in the dictionary" ...certainly, I would feel honored by this and thanked Lorraine while we both chuckled.

Many scholars say Shakespeare's allusion choices spread personal, romantic, historical, allegorical, spiritual and philosophical enrichments throughout his work. A more recent young scholar, Daniel Swift in his 2013 Oxford University Press book, *Shakespeare's Common Prayers: The Book of Common Prayer and the Elizabethan Age*, for 280 plus pages examines how influential the BCP was on Shakespeare's life & work. When referring to *Sonnet 23* (p. 78) he states generally: "The sonnets are games of form and articulation: they are about what truth may be boxed in set speech. Here the truest speaker is an actor, straining for the words of his role." Swift transitions (p. 79) to the sonnet embedded in Romeo and Juliet's dialogue, "upon meeting" they "speak instantly of holiness" as if a direct embodiment of the prayer book's influence:

> ROMEO: If I profane with my unworthiest hand
>
> This holy shrine, the gentler sin is this:
>
> My lips, two blushing pilgrims, ready stand
>
> To smooth that rough touch with a tender kiss.
>
> JULIET: Good pilgrim, you do wrong your hand too much,
>
> Which mannerly devotion shows in this.
>
> For saints have hands that pilgrims' hands too touch,
>
> And palm to palm is holy palmers' kiss.
>
> ROMEO: Have not saints lips, and holy palmers, too?
>
> JULIET: Ay, pilgrim, lips that they must use in prayer.
>
> ROMEO: O then, dear saint, let lips do what hands do:
>
> They pray; grant thou, lest faith turn to despair.
>
> JULIET: Saints do not move, though grant for prayers' sake.
>
> ROMEO: Then move not while my prayer's effect I take.
> (1.5.90-103)

211

Shakespeare's Wake, was first planned to have 22 crowns and does with a twist: 21 with 7 sonnets (some with variations on crown form), a 3 sonnet epiphany "crown-et" and 4 more epilogue "allusion" sonnets making 154 with allusions throughout from all 154 in Shakespeare's collection. There are 10 "transition" sonnets (not for numbered allusions) as intros and exits, all totaling 164 sonnets. Volume 2, *Recycling the Circle*, now with 3 crowns, epiphany crown and 58 sonnets (with variations) has 82. Volume 3, *Romance Languages*, first had a garland and crown with 54 sonnets, to total 300 (double the number of Bible psalms) in the trilogy. From 4th volume new sonnets, 2nd and 3rd's vols. may be added to later for a more conceptually complete trilogy. The 300 was suggested intuitively by an editor friend at the time before the trilogy concept arose, it may as yet infer as well on the trilogy process. It will not be surprising to count the final number of "allusion sonnets" at completion and find there are 300, 304 or 308. A doubling of *Shakespeare's Sonnets* concept occurred early on when compiling the tribute idea before a trilogy revealed itself while writing through a crown series and before considering Coverdale psalm allusions in *Shakespeare's Sonnets*.

The 3 volumes contain tragedies, comedies, myth allusions, some pieces include blends of romance, history and comedy like compressed inner "shake-scene play-lets." Heroic sonnet forms express the obvious and the indescribable as unified active imagination. In this way a rose is never just a rose. Separate books, B & W and color, with individual covers & illustrations may serve volume distinctions better for some readers.

The last revision process planned Shakespeare sonnet allusions for each line, with alluded from sonnet numbers in brackets beside titles or numbers of the poems. Allusion numbers for volumes 2 & 3 seem more erratic due to sequence change developments mentioned earlier. Original number schemes for allusions tended to work out even after revised sonnet position changes. Two 16 sonnet dual redouble' forms were dropped. Next some revealing rigor is examined.

The dual redouble' is my extension of the form with an "index" sonnet at each end, sonnet 1 and 16. The eliminations changed a predetermined sequence of how sonnet allusions would come from Shakespeare's numbered sonnets in a 1-154 count for each of mine, as in a "same numbered" sequence. Removing the first redouble' from vol. 1 and the second from vol. 2, improved the end result when keeping the three best sonnets of the first redouble' and spreading them out in vol. 2, while reducing the other redouble' to a 7 sonnet crown and moving it to the epilogue of vol. 1, with Coverdale psalm allusions also added (as Shakespeare used, several even in the same numbered psalm as sonnet, these details are described in my essay *Shakespeare's Operatic Crown*). The goal of numbered allusions italicized in each line is to be more "revealing" than the Bard's allusions being discretely, secretively imbedded or even coded.

Exploring led to Coverdale allusions as well as sonnet allusions in 3 crowns. Sonnets for allusions were not to be used more than once in each of the separate volumes but in volumes 2 and 3, a few repetitive sonnet allusion numbers seemed necessary. The reasons for repeating the numbers had to do with revision, placement changes like those described before, altering the predetermined numerical arrangement with new poems, and not merely due to random choice or similar thematic content. I lost track of how vol. 2 allusions began with #66, it probably had to do with the "recycling" need to repeat an allusion pattern & counting all 164 sonnets in vol. 1 while dropping the "100," then skipping the intro sonnet of vol. 2 with no allusions. This would compensate also for changes, as in the opening section line up, thus beginning vol. 2 with Shakespeare's #66 for allusions. Sonnet number ordering for allusions in vol. 2 felt at times like mixing watercolors, tuning a guitar or consulting the *I-Ching* with yarrow sticks, found in the Bollingen translation with Carl Jung's *Synchronicity Forward*. A numerical and not thematic approach for sonnet selections for allusion was used to add an element of mystery.

The 3 volume single book published with the new pen name seemed to develop its own kind of "artificial Shakespeare intelligence" due to more considerations than merely an allusion scheme, placement changes and revision. Though intuitive adjustments in vol. 1's order and how Shakespeare's 1-154 allusion sonnets lined up to the epilogue slightly changed after revisions, how vol. 1's placements led to vol. 2 and vol. 3, may have mystified C. G. Jung more than Joseph Campbell (or vise-a-versa!). The allusion process was set not to use a word or phrase more than once or more times than had been used by Shakespeare in the particular sonnet choice (#42 has 7 "love" root word uses, #40 has 10!). Not over using allusions also extended to Coverdale psalms in 3 crowns. Some later revisions (as in *Stephen Hawking's Mythology of Everything; ASAP: Age of the Second Adam's Paradigm* and the transition sonnets) did not work well with systematic allusion plans for each line without completely rewriting the poems, so were left unchanged & unnumbered.

The allusion sequence for vol. 3 did not stem from how vol. 2 developed but extended from the pattern of a group of nine non-consecutive Shakespeare sonnet numbers listed in a row by author Gerald Massey in the 1888 book, *The Secret Drama of Shakespeare's Sonnets Unfolded* (p. 205 - 210). His narrative sequence involves different characters in what appears to be an operatic relationship struggle. Massey elaborates on the narrative involving Shakespeare "friends" with clarifying detail fit for a courtroom drama, almost as if he had known the characters personally! Vol. 3, *Romance Languages*, is a romantic psycho-comedy with an ending twist conceptually like a crown of sonnets ties back into volume 1. Vol. 1 deals with romance in the beginning section and later curves before the epilogue, into the Orpheus myth that blends everything from visionary dream epiphany to modern gothic horror, historical, dramatic, psychological and mythical/alchemical sequences. Comedic relief like pixie dust is generously sprinkled through various parts of the trilogy aided and abetted by all the rhyming and no blank verse.

Even Shakespeare deviated from strict use of iambic pentameter from first to last syllable at times. I tried to be faithfully aware of the metrical sound of lines throughout even when variations were used. As the essay conclusions reached the "operatic essence" of the Bard's sonnets before discovering Gerald Massey's "unfolding" concept, it was amusing and bracing to find Massey's similar reading. From Massey's nearly absurd to clairvoyant-like detective work, his determination helped spur on the arduous task of rewriting to include, as a more challenging tribute, a numbered pattern of Shakespeare sonnet allusions that would "puzzle through" each line like a strange parlor game for modern "nobles." The turn the volumes took after allusions were set up resulted in very challenging, often puzzling results, but never failed to intrigue, amaze and/or amuse. Turn to the last four sonnets in the Bard's series, listen for the humor that circulates there and try to imagine what it may have sounded like to the clever English dry witted ears of his readers at that time. The Bard exhibited the hallmarks of elevated comedy in sonnets as in plays, perhaps more concentrated in the sonnets, as in his sonnet series last lines, "Came there for cure, and this by that I prove / Love's fire heats water, water cools not love," as the epitome of dry English wit.

The allusion-sonnet order for vol. 3, repeated in an extending cyclical pattern, Massey's narrative sequence of nine sonnets that were according to him (like opera) set to specific music (p. 210), that of Autolycus's music to *Two Maids Wooing a Man* and are listed in this specific order (144, 33, 34, 35, 41, 42, 133, 134, 40). Samples of his comments, are referred to and examined at the end of the essay *Shakespeare's Operatic Crown* which follows: "After offering eloquent investigative evidence like a trial lawyer, Massey points out characters Shakespeare knew and veiled in the Sonnets with their personal traits and dramatic motives:"

"Elizabeth Vernon's jealousy of her lover the Earl of Southampton and her friend and cousin Lady Rich, is told in these nine sonnets, which are now for the first time put together: they go to Autolycus's tune of *Two Maids Wooing a Man*. The first sonnet contains a soliloquy on the subject, a form employed more than once in the dramatic Sonnets. Then we have five Sonnets addressed to the Earl, and three to the lady of whom Elizabeth Vernon is jealous (Lady Rich) (p. 210-11)."

Autolycus, the ballad selling rogue in *The Winter's Tale*, 4.4.286-89, refers to a merry ballad which "...goes to the tune of *Two Maids Wooing a Man*." "There's scarce a maid westward but she sings it. Tis in request, I can tell you." Massey seems to know the tune enough to capitalize on it in 1888. By 2017, Catherine Henze in her book *Robert Armin and Shakespeare's Performed Songs*, refers to the song among others also sung by Armin as Autolycus. She notes the lyrics but not the music came down to us (as Autolycus' other song melodies did) (p. 84). In 1599, Armin, also a writer (*Quips for Questions*) was hired as a musician/actor by Shakespeare for the Chamberlain's Men and took the primary roll of the fool (p.1).

Regarding the veiled sonnet characters named by Massey, it is compelling to see the Lady Penelope Rich saga Massey lays out with Sir Philip Sidney's connection (p. 352-6) is also brought out in agreement but with more emphasis on Sidney, by Clare Asquith in 2005's *Shadowplay* (p. 151). Massey compiled such a thorough dossier on Lady Rich's beauty that perhaps even Cleopatra's beauty received less notice by Shakespeare. Massey argues at length that Lady Rich, the first love (though unrequited) of Sir Sidney, was the model for Shakespeare's later Dark Lady sonnets (after #126 and earlier) as well as being Sidney's 'chiaroscuro' eyed inspiration for Stella (p. 356). Professor Bloom in 2011's *The Anatomy of Influence*, in the chapter: *Possession In Many Modes: The Sonnets,* (p. 83) mentions the doubling and tripling of possible source figures referred to in certain sonnet figures such as the Dark Lady and the Rival Poet.

Clare Asquith compiles a similarly weighty analysis of Sir Sidney being the linchpin model/influence for the character and voice of Hamlet from several aspects included in his books: *A Defense of Poesie, Arcadia* and his epic sonnet sequence *Astrophel and Stella*, as well as the facts and legendary points of interest pertaining to Sydney's English nobility and death at 32 by an infected thigh wound in a described indecisive/useless action (p. 147-52). Clare Asquith refers to *A Defense of Poetry* as: "...colloquial, graceful, at once casual and learnedly authoritative, in the witty tradition of Erasmus and Montaigne... a bastion of common sense, written in reply to a critic on the theatre...." Lady Rich, according to Asquith, as "the beautiful and intelligent sister of Essex (who was beheaded for treason), as an active member of his dissident circle," was one who "...may have been providing acceptable cover for poetry that was in fact political and religious" in aiding Catholics. Lady Asquith points out Sidney's writings as: "elaborately allegorical, (that) suggest a gradual disillusion with English Protestantism, and a growing sympathy with the plight of Catholicism" (p. 149).

Turning to Sir Sidney's "Petrarchan" sonnet sequence *Astrophel and Stella,* from which allusions may be seen in Hamlet's voice & divided character and in other plays like *Richard III*, the basic idea is found there for a monumental Shakespeare sonnet sequence. Parallels can be found in Sidney's lines: Sonnet 69.7, "Gone is the Winter of my miserie!" calling to mind *Richard III*'s, "Now is the winter of our discontent." Hamlet's echo can be heard in Sidney's Sonnet 68.10: "Labour to kill in me this killing care" and Sonnet 69.14, "No kings be crown'd but they some covenants make." Music allusions are found in *Astrophel and Stella*: Sonnet 68.6 on Stella: "With voice more fit to wed Amphion's lyre," for his Muse in Sonnet 70.3-6:

> She oft hath drunk my tears, now hopes to enjoy
>
> Nectar of mirth, since I love's cup do keep
>
> Sonnets be not bound Prentice to annoy;
>
> Trebles sing high, so well as basses deep;

Then 70.9-14 ends with:

> Come then, my Muse, shew thou height of delight
>
> In well raised notes; my pen, the best it may,
>
> Shall paint out joy, though in but black and white.
>
> Cease, eager Muse; peace, pen, for my sake stay,
>
> I give you here my hand for truth of this,
>
>
> Wise silence is best musicke unto blisse.

Having achieved the romantic equivalence of "rock star" status after death, Sir Sidney's ending verse here even calls to mind Hamlet's fitting epitaph: "The rest is silence" called to Horatio who bears out with "Good night, sweet prince, / And flights of angels sing thee to thy rest." This strangely calls to mind the strange and contrasting agitated interlude with the afterlife summons of their "ghost meeting interaction outcome" where Hamlet addresses a nearly manic episode (as modeling the mania himself!) marked by Horatio's "wondrous strange!" exclamation:

> And therefore as a stranger give it welcome.
>
> There are more things in heaven and earth, Horatio,
>
> Than are dreamt of in your philosophy. But come,
>
> Here as before, never, so help you mercy,
>
> How strange or odd soe'er I bear myself-
>
> As I perchance hereafter shall think meet

to put an antic disposition on-

That you at such time seeing me never shall,

With arms encumbered thus, or this headshake,

Or by pronouncing of some doubtful phrase

As 'Well, we know' or 'We could an 'if we would',

Or 'If we list to speak', or 'There be an 'if they might',

Or such ambiguous giving out, to note

That you know aught of me- this not to do,

So grace and mercy at your most need help you, swear.

GHOST: (under the stage) Swear.

[They swear] (1.5.167-182)

Before it has all sunk in, Hamlet starts in a reasoned manner and dis-position to rationally reassure Horatio, their reactions are not madness but normal when overwhelmed at the thought of what was just experi-enced. He bids them to keep calm and not strike up excitement, not to wonder of weirdness in him or themselves, then gets into a monologue riff that in turn goes antic; breathtakingly rippling words surge into an oath forced on them of how not to act and what not to do until the clang of the final ordering word "swear," which is suddenly echoed much deeper by the invisible ghost with an ambiguously "wondrous strange" comedic effect as if in complete support from the gate of the underworld, demandingly perturbed, reinforcing moral conscience on the way back to the under(stage)world in unrest, not to be forgotten & sworn by them in echo.

Considering Massey's sonnet list order, 33 with ambiguous heavy alle-gorical landscape imagery, "glorious morning," then spiritual allusions of "celestial face" and "heaven's sun," sounds like a more fitting soliloquy or overture than 144. Line 11 of 33, plays loss off on the allegory in a climactic outburst: "But, out! alack! he was but one hour mine," on to end, "heaven's sun staineth." The list goes on fine through 134, then 144 would return to the allegorical images of 33 as a romantic struggle with "good & bad angels." Lastly, 40 bids for an overwhelming conflict reso-lution hope with "love" used 10 times! Clare Asquith in her "Selection of Coded Terms" (p. 299) refers to 33 as alluding to Christ's passion and age of death and the age Shakespeare was when his son Hamnet died, which seems most fitting to bear the grandest allegorical and transcen-dent soliloquy weight of his Sonnets series. As John Keats in a letter referred to Shakespeare possessing virtually unlimited amounts of "nega-tive capability," both appear to have made just as much use of active in-ference to quell free energy risks & dissipations in their lines to achieve sublime "simplified intensities" as Yeats sees fit to name & comprehend such transcendent consciousness issues.

An interesting relative passage in Dr. Harold Bloom's, *A Map of Mis-reading*, (p. 67) refers to Milton's "power of religious phenomenology:" "As a man, evidently he was Christian (of his own sect, a sect of one) but as poet he was a fierce Miltonist, and as much a son of himself as of God. If the imagination, in poetry, speaks of itself, then it speaks of ori-gins, of the archaic, of the primal, and above all of self-preservation." Next examining Vico's "magic formalism" used as a tool of the "self-defining function of imagination," Dr. Bloom refers to Auerbach's sum-mary: "The aim of primitive imagination... is not liberty but... establish-ment of fixed limits, as a psychological and material protection against the chaos of the surrounding world." Thank you Dr. Bloom, several of these aspects mentioned in both passages resonate throughout *Shake-speare's Sonnets* as well as the general structure and purpose of my "quadrilogy."

The deaths of friends, Guy Charleville, followed by Susan Austell less than a month later, spurred a series of dreams, inquires, new poems, revi-sions of old poems and an essay resulting in a 4th volume, now: *Radio Waves Color Blind,* that condenses the "quadrilogy" into a book of essen-tial thematic sonnets, prints & essays. New sonnets seemed to come to me like the dreams of dead and living friends, in 3's. The 2nd major essay seemed to beg on a 3rd essay that would go full circle, back to the original trilogy idea and would address the "AI" aspect of the title more fully …this third essay is the fruit of that search for understanding more lucidly, the unfolding work of expanding consciousness and imagination. It contains major elements of two longer essays and shorter descriptive ending pieces of previous appendices: *Forming the Trilogy* and the *Afterword*. Essential parts for a more thorough exploration of the trilogy goals were used to ex-pand awareness of ideas relative to new "AI concepts & jargon" presented in essays by and about Dr. Karl Friston's working "Active Inference –AI" ideas. While considering his statements on AI and consciousness in con-cert with other prominent published thinkers, ideas of ethics and con-sciousness arose as paramount issues.

For example, Dr. Henry Kissinger's essay in the June 2018, Atlantic (p. 13-14) maintained, "The most difficult yet important question about the world in which we are headed is this: What will become of human con-sciousness if its own explanatory power is surpassed by AI, and societies are no longer able to interpret the world they inhabit in terms that are meaningful to them? How is consciousness to be defined in a world of machines that reduce human experience to mathematical data, interpreted by their own memories?" Aspects of this struggle using metrical forms & codes engaged sonneteers of the Enlightenment like Sir Sidney and Shakespeare, perhaps only meaningful to a small group, though Shakespeare "numbers" expanded into a cottage industry over the years. This 3rd essay of my trilogy/quadrilogy addresses some issues previously stated in the awareness of numeric rhythmical structures and no matter how flawed or menial it may appear to some, this "trilogy machine" has a quality of inevitability. The longer it is around to be engaged with, like each day, it is and is not a surprise, it was and is an active inference (AI) to the next day and essays into it.. thanks to Professor Friston's Free Energy Principle work, my work fits the theory as a predicted outcome in itself.

The pattern aspect of all three volumes, examined in the appendix piece, *Forming the Trilogy,* reduces free energy scatterings in use of active inference patterned models. The resulting outcome of the allusion process, bolstered by three essays, amplifies the work's aura of an artificial Shakespeare intelligence. Illuminated by the current expanding essay, which could conceivably go on as a kind of "essay unlimited" thanks to influences of critics like Professor Harold Bloom, with further exploring or in "Fristonese: epistemic foraging" (*Wired,* Dec. 2018, p. 103) this work continues to grow. Writing is a display of consciousness that believes in something or it has no reason or purpose to be written but to be its own stain on paper like randomly moving bugs under a covering log of decomposition moving faster in the light.

This active inference AI works with belief systems in which whatever inferred influence ones anxiety yields itself to or is drawn to ..or with "no-belief," yet another form of belief system. At what point is point of view merely a matter of semantics where clinical, scientific, philosophical, theological, observational inference becomes faith in what's next? How does ones subjective "proof-self" prove outcomes in these matters of "what is simply is," as Friston's bugs proved to him, fulfilling the "new AI" ..with the same knowing that produces the least amount of statistical error while reducing "free energy," in such a way that wins AI software development contests & hopeful best sellers?

While considering Professor Karl Friston's insights with as much gravitas as Freud or Jung's dream work in regard to my sonnet project and its processes, without getting into specific belief systems that would doubtlessly result in an agon of conflicting opinions Dr. Bloom would instantly recall, which Professor Friston would in all probability just as quickly recoil from in my findings or approach, as perhaps flirting with aspects of dementia or some psychosis according to his clinically correct Markov blanket approach, keeping his "existence for existence sake" scientific ethos "safety-net" intact ..I still find myself out on the limb of gratitude and bow to his noble exploratory discourses and commitments while maintaining my own unconditional positive regard.

As for reducing the "free energy" around my sonnet project in order to evolve 'higher' from its kernel of love through devotion to Shakespearian purposes of that "promised eternity" in the dedication of his "unlimited sonnet crown," so that his work is prophetic of my own, mine actively infers itself into a self-fulfilling prophecy of its own enlightened entanglement with Shakespeare, Bloom, Friston & beyond. My 1st college poetry writing teacher, John Gery, in his critique of my epic, *Why John Lennon Died for My Sins*, (granted the irony may be lost on most readers but the shocking generality of the title was enough to spur the imagination & generate attention) in Spring '81, cued me up to a purpose of individual 'sect of one' belief system conceptualizations a la' Yeats's *A Vision*, right out of the starting gate.

Ten years later he offered to sponsor me through continuation of an MFA program in writing I had completed the majority of. Very gracious but with a masters degree in counseling secured, I opted to drop out, tune in & turn on my own pace, the results being this life's journey approach. My course of study was not offered at the university per say unless it was to be another General Studies degree multi-media art plan. It would take time to pan out artful pursuits while earning a living as an art teacher married to a librarian. There were a lot of "free energy" fires to reduce along the way of underestimated authorial strengths while coming into my own as a visual artist, musician, videographer, writer, including a pen name & trademarked occupation as publisher ..everything else seemed to have to fall away for its maximum realization.

It was then back to Yeats in a more confident ways of distilling his "pluses & minuses." Any love lacking in Yeats's "cold eye" view is made up for in Shakespeare, Whitman & Dickinson. Yet they did not see myth-busting 'mathematical-mechanical paradigm extremes' Yeats faced (to world wars) focused on in Patrick Keane's essay: *Yeats's Counter-Enlightenment*, in *Salmagundi* (1985; p. 126). The pessimism Yeats bore toward the Locke-Newton paradigm cycled through the inability of humans as a whole, to combine the natural & supernatural competently & transcendently in an 'AI' of the "mirror turned lamp" soul's past-myth-connected "active imagination," for the Enlightenment's high Romantic cure (p. 136). Informed more by the dead, who were not dead, ironically more alive than most humans, Yeats inferred his belief system through a spousal induced medium that yielded the book, *A Vision*. How could his classical hero paradigm be replaced by AI's post-war journey, of cold mathematical abstractions that would enable man's "one giant leap for mankind" paradigm of baby-steppers-in-space hubris, to that 'hollow moon' while keeping a finger poised over the nuclear MAD (mutual assured destruction) button? Will AI take the place of that finger? "Yeats's coming" had "come round at last" to know his Homeric heroes inferred the same.

What higher purpose could AI possibly have, when accounting for belief systems as forms of consciousness, other than crunching "cold-blooded" numbers.. besides inferring and reaffirming a projected faith in life after death as the most profound conclusion of human consciousness and its end results? Why did Socrates seem pleased to drink the hemlock?

The symbols sparkle in the lights all around us, even in what we can not see and this writing is one more example going forward into the lights, darkness, mists, to beyond the veil. My work appears, from the start, if not having evolved from higher consciousness, as I believe it has, to bare fruit of "new" AI hallmarks in exploration, reasoned & random risks, bestowals & gains, losses & discoveries, journeys.. Lee Circle to Lin Emery's Circle, in dreams & awake with this new Shakespeare (active inference) AI.

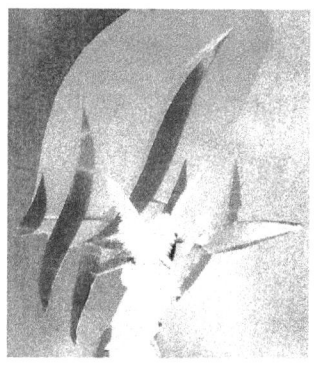

Afterword

The 2016 essay on his Sonnets, marked the 400 year death anniversary of Shakespeare and caused reimagining this text as a more thorough tribute. Tulane University professor and Louisiana State Poet Laureate, Peter Cooley, hosted the Sonnet part of a month long series of anniversary events called "First Folio!" The 2016 elaborate production featured readings, recitals, plays, displays of period publications of plays, poems, the *Sonnets* and an actual *First Folio* opened to *Hamlet* under a Plexiglas cube in Tulane's newly established Newcomb Art Museum.

My trilogy tribute idea with allusions emerged after the essay research. One volume combining the essay and the 3 separate volumes seemed a worthy tribute at 300 sonnets (or a doubling of *Shakespeare's Sonnets* I had in mind even before advised 5 years earlier to round the contents down to 300, from approximately twice that, by a poet/editor/teacher friend, Ralph Adamo). Reading the essay one can see where the allusion idea came from and what motivations Shakespeare may have had in allusion usage considering the importance of English Bible translations. All Coverdale's translated 150 psalms of *The Book of Psalms* still remain in England's *Book of Common Prayer*.

The formal high modern English with which Shakespeare was well acquainted to the point of being dramatically responsible for its vocabulary expansion through his writing, was based on a good grounding in the holy scriptures, mythology and readings throughout the liberal arts, in law as well as good grammar and Latin education. My own research over the years in a liberal arts education, masters degree in counseling, masters studies in art history and creative writing as part of an MFA curriculum in poetry and independent studies in the English Bible, immersion in documentary films repeated regularly on cable's *History Channel, YouTube* videos and the PBS television network, have added to the development of comprehension skills that assisted in propelling me to achieve these poetic works and enlightened thoughts.

Though the title, *Shakespeare AI,* may seem a misnomer, it is a catchy "iconcurchaic" one that may afford some stimulation to the poetic memory banks in order to purchase its license worth of parody as well as profundity. One of the bravest challenge pursuits was to include the allusions throughout the trilogy which required a complete revision of the text. Due to the allusion process the work takes on an even more profound aspect of an "artificial Shakespeare intelligence" which is how the title transformation into *Shakespeare AI* was justified. The title was lastly and strangely aided and abetted by a curious essay in *The Atlantic* magazine, "How the Enlightenment Ends: Philosophically, intellectually

–in every way –human society is unprepared for the rise of artificial intelligence" by Dr. Henry A. Kissinger (June 2018). The cover headline refers to it as: *AI and the End of Human History* (quite an opposite bookend to Dr. Harold Bloom's published concept of *Shakespeare: the Invention of the Human*!)

The title *Shakespeare's Wake*, chosen for volume one, came from one of Dr. Harold Bloom's descriptions of James Joyce's *Finnegans Wake* (A. of I., p. 112). In one concluding poem, *ASAP,* (last sonnet in 1st of 3 versions of the trilogy) some key words were also inspired by Dr. Bloom, from passages in his 1996 book on "The Gnosis of Angels, Dreams, and Resurrection," *Omens of Millennium.* It is interesting to note that I had not read enough of the book for it to consciously influence the writing of the trilogy before its final poem. I was excited to find several correlations in our use of words and ideas while recently reading his book more deeply. A current version of the poem *ASAP* uses the words: "archon" and "Pleroma" from his splendorous book (p. 239-40).

The term "iconcurchaic," my invention as a tribute to the Parisian poet/critic (friend of Picasso) G. Apollinaire, as well as the Bard, means something iconic and current while also being archaic, with an implication of timelessness. I hope this book imparts the same to the reader, in various ways not excluding irony, as well as an enriched interest in Shakespeare's work and methods which may lend some forbearance of judgment for readers against the strangeness of my book, who can not read it with the "Negative Capability" of Keats in mind (of which in a letter Keats wrote:

"Shakespeare possessed enormously"). Though this book at times resembles curious best seller oddities such as Calvin Parker's 2018 book, *Pascagoula-The Closest Encounter: My Story*, about his and Charles Hickson's night fishing trip alien abduction experience in 1973, my efforts are validated by pieces under my name & pen name on the current (2019) Pirate's Alley, Rosemary James and Joseph DeSalvo produced, Faulkner-Wisdom literary contest finalist and short lists.

To bear the Bard's all-encompassing insight toward Horatio's "wondrous strange!" remark upon the interaction of the men with Hamlet's father's ghost, he has Hamlet say:

And therefore as a stranger give it welcome.

There are more things in heaven and earth, Horatio,

Than are dreamt of in our philosophy.

(1.5.167-169)

The artist Lin Emery gave the three book effort a thrilling statement (extracted from here) pertaining to my use of her sublime metaphorical sculpture *Flight* in the composite photographs for the covers of the trilog *Shakespeare AI* and Vol. 2, *Recycling the Circle*, when emailing after an hour meditation session with the Dali Lama's personal physician: "Your overwhelming poems were a fitting coda... Thank you for including me in your Circles!" What an exquisitely gracious "Zen-engineering artist" she is of the spirit as well as metal.

In 2000 I dreamed of her sculpture *Flight* being on the column instead of Lee at Lee Circle in New Orleans. *Flight* once stood in a perfectly proportioned reflecting pool with exquisite lily pads, lotuses and goldfish, to grace the front of NOMA, the Museum of Art, a favorite New Orleans structure and setting. I regard it as the museum façade's crowning sculpture that has unfortunately been removed to the shadowy realms of the museum's rearwards "sculpture garden" like a UFO landing in a manicured swamp. The dream inspired my photographic "odd-yssey" in 2000 in which a narrative series took shape from "double exposures" of her sculpture and the top of the Lee Circle column (as well as other combinations after seeing the beginning results) with 35mm film in an "auto-everything" Nikon camera.

The process resulted in a 2016 *Recycling the Circle* cover idea, with a framed print presented to Mayor Mitch Landrieu (at his 2018 book signing of, *In the Shadow of Statues*) to which he remarked "That's beautiful!" I then mentioned my dream of Lin's sculpture on Lee's column and thought it could then be called Lin Emery Circle. Though he had removed the statue for an appropriate setting such as a cemetery or museum, he said renaming Lee Circle was not for him to decide.

Lin's deep reflections will remain greatly appreciated with hopes that one day her sculpture *Flight* will be returned to its sublime place in the reflecting pool to crown the beautiful facade of the New Orleans Museum of Art, as only it seems to grace with such unique mysterious excellence that changes, like & with nature. As this book enters the world with care here's hoping it will help enrich lives of readers for a deeper appreciation of *Shakespeare's Sonnets* & his volume's dedication on behalf of the Bard's "promised eternity," proclaimed to delighted open minds.

M. D. V.

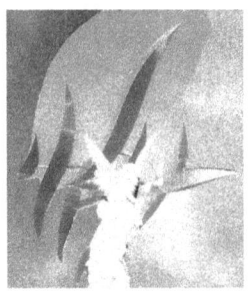

Epithalamic Epilogue & Epitaph

In response to loving critics who work behind me, beside me or who merely love from a distance, themselves as wedded well, but may not know how "good," or those who expect me at the altar of ego or no-go (when what I have is difficult enough to marry without the eternal bridegroom's betrothal), for them this consolation prize. To critics who weigh me in their scales of learned ignorance more blind than the flip side of justice to their own blindness, thin kings of my flittering hybrid's fat stunted imagination, I dedicate to their degrees of "word zymurgy maya" what could have been thoughts of Hamlet to detractors had he survived (as he does here), I leave their cool pomposity the parting point of Sonnet 121:

> 'Tis better to be vile than vile esteemed,
> When not to be receives reproach of being;
> And the just pleasure lost, which is so deemed
> Not by our feeling, but by others' seeing:
> For why should others' false adulterate eyes
> Give salutation to my sportive blood?
> Or on my frailties why are frailer spies,
> Which in their wills count bad what I think good?
> No, I am that I am, and they that level
> At my abuses reckon up their own:
> I may be straight though they themselves be bevel;
> By their rank thoughts my deeds must not be shown;
> Unless this general evil they maintain,
> All men are bad and in their badness reign.

Besides a Psalm (Coverdale's 116: "All men are liars"), this also calls to mind Hamlet's concluding remarks on actor treatment: "better have a bad epitaph than their ill report while you live" (2.2.528-9).

So here is mine now:

> My ardent spirits do not desert me now for fear
> of drinking from bridal glass or last supper cup,
> my book's feast serves both scholar & common reader
> may it serve you well with both hands to follow up.

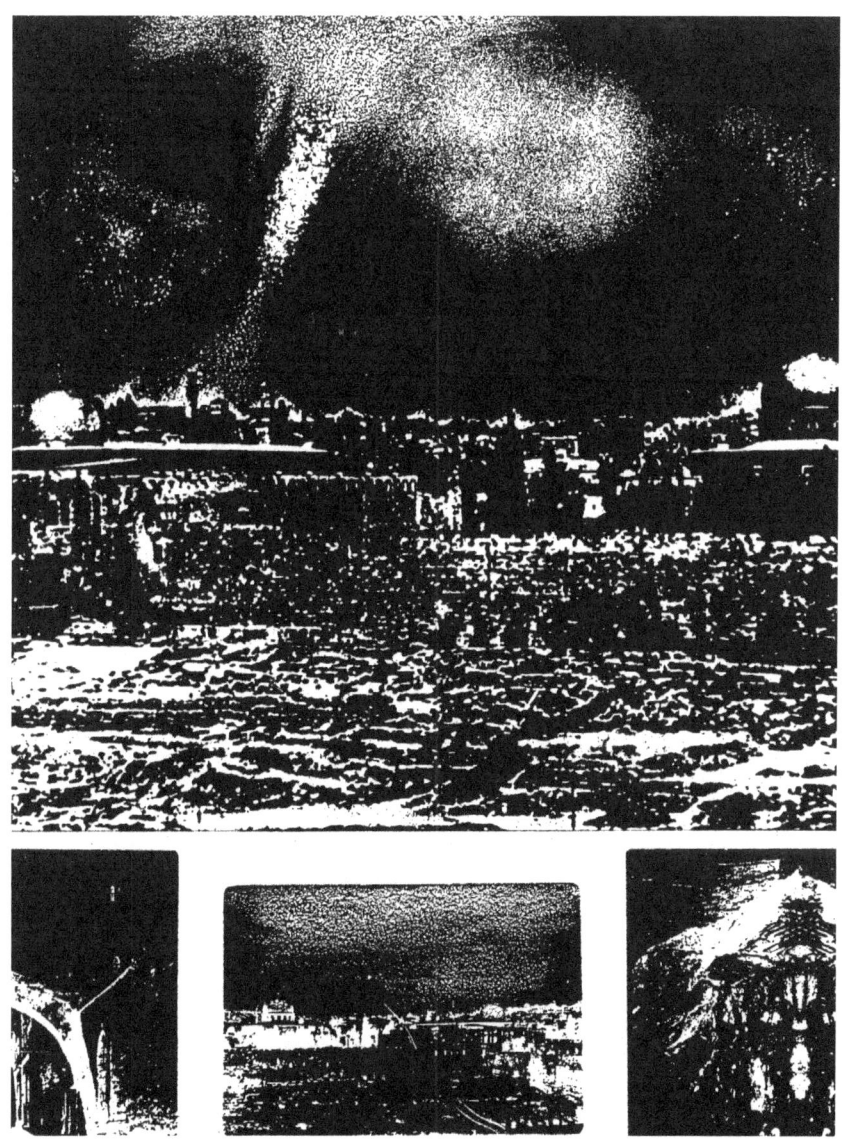

streaming: www.bontonrepublic.com

Bon Ton Amore'

Running Downtown with Sal
La Belle Orleanna Evergreen
Kentucky Derby Day
Once Upon Tomorrow
Gypsy Rhapsody
Her Roses Arrive
Safe Secrets
Chances Are
Wingback Rider
She Walks in Beauty
You Are My Light (Slow Burn)
Beyond Measure
You Are My Light
Eldorado Rhapsody (Day Dream)

M. D. Veritas

All instruments M. D. Veritas except Salvador Carlino, double bass on Running Downtown with Sal & You Are My Light

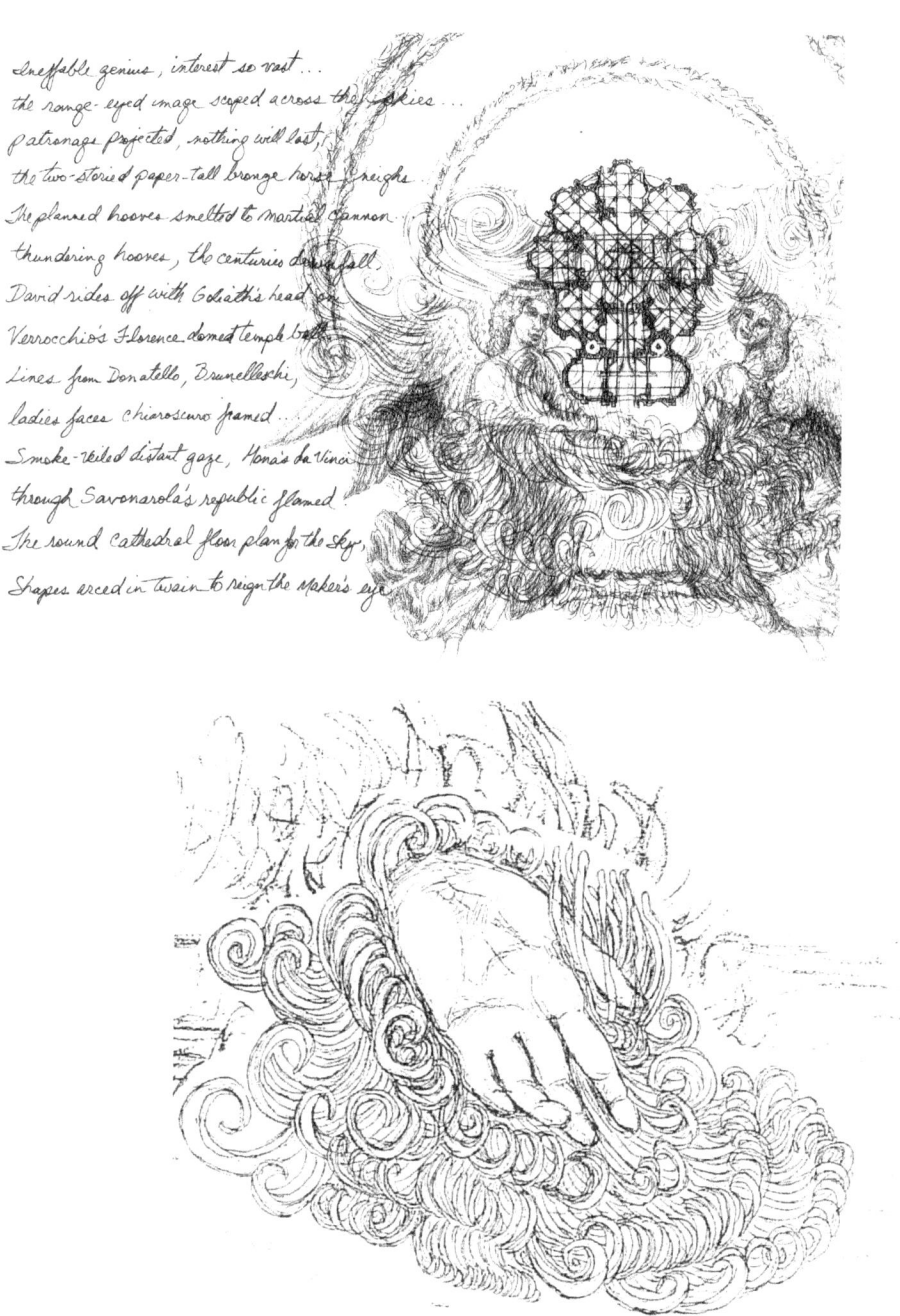

Ineffable genius, interest so vast...
the range-eyed image scoped across the skies...
patronage projected, nothing will last,
the two-storied paper-tall bronze horse neighs.
The planned hooves smelted to martial cannon
thundering hooves, the centuries downfall.
David rides off with Goliath's head
Verrocchio's Florence domed temple bath
Lines from Donatello, Brunelleschi,
ladies faces chiaroscuro framed...
Smoke-veiled distant gaze, Mona's da Vinci
through Savonarola's republic flamed
The round cathedral floor plan for the sky,
Shapes arced in twain to reign the maker's eye

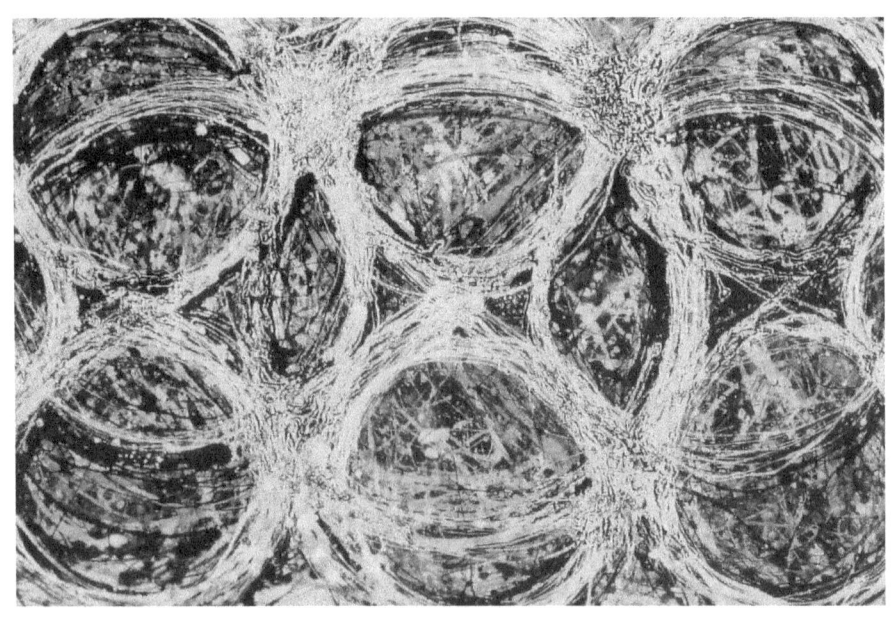

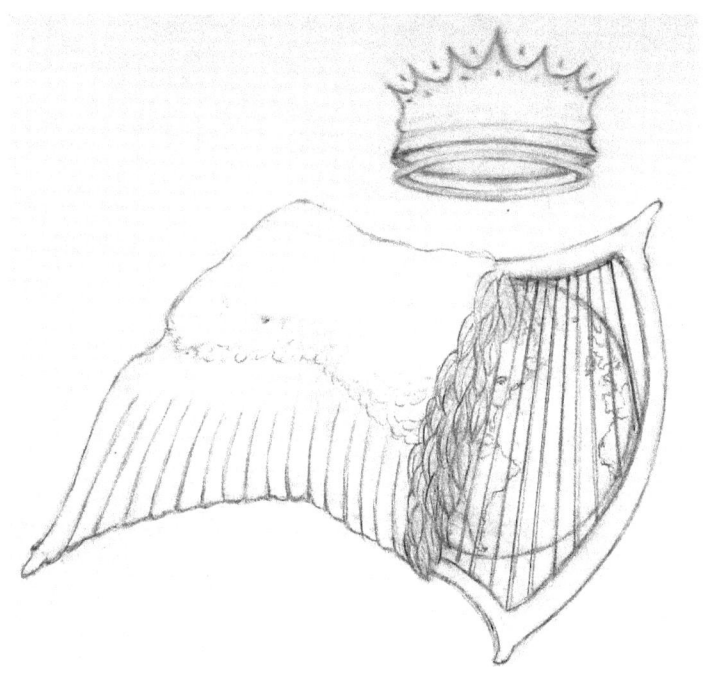